at last,
The Real Distinguished Thing

at last,

The Real Distinguished Thing

The Late Poems of Eliot, Pound, Stevens, and Williams

by Kathleen Woodward

OHIO STATE UNIVERSITY PRESS

Copyright © 1980 by the Ohio State University Press
All rights reserved
Manufactured in the United States of America

Library of Congress Cataloging in Publication Data
Woodward, Kathleen M.   At last, the real distinguished thing
Includes bibliographical references and index
1. American poetry—20th century—History and criticism. 2. Aged in literature. I. Title
PS310.A34W6   811'.52'09   80-23126
ISBN 0-8142-0306-X

To Roy Harvey Pearce

Contents

PREFACE

Gertrude Stein's last words were cast in the wry and questioning style of Postmodernism. "What is the answer?" she asked, and receiving only an empty silence, pressed further: "What is the question?" But this book takes as its title not the last words of Stein, which throw us off balance, but those of the great Modern writer Henry James. "At last," he is quoted as saying, "the real distinguished thing." The sober tone, the sense of final achievement and discovery, the poise of authoritative endings, the judiciousness and breadth of perspective— these are the qualities that interest me.

In recent years, my research and teaching has been concerned with the distinctions between Modernism and Postmodernism in American literature and the problems of aging and the elderly in our century's industrial culture. The latter takes many people by surprise. I am often asked how I became interested in doing research on old age with the materials and methods of the humanities. There are, of course, many answers to this question, all of which have personal dimensions and some of which are no doubt reflected in this book, although I must confess that I realize this only in retrospect. For the conception of this book evolved over a long period of time. I did not in fact set out consciously to write a book on aging and poetry, although this is just what has emerged.

The process began simply enough. Some seven years ago, while reading the poetry of Wallace Stevens, I found myself drawn to his last poems, preferring them to the early poems of *Harmonium* and subsequent volumes at a time when his last poems had received comparatively little critical attention and the early poems were canonized. I decided to study them in the context of the entire body of Stevens' work to discover if I could account for a development over time. I also was concerned to understand the place of these poems—an old man's poems—in our cultural history. Did they, I wondered, offer our culture a model for the satisfactions which I felt? And were Stevens' achievements paralleled elsewhere? I turned to William Carlos Williams, whose major last work was published about the same time. *Paterson V* is critical to the comprehension of Williams' development as a poet; it extends his most ambitious poem while at the same time departing significantly from it, testifying to a poetic and personal crisis which involved both Williams' loss of power in old age and issues of tradition and authority. Was the coincidence of *The Rock* and *Paterson V,* so similar in many respects, an accident? If not, what did this reveal not just about individual poetic development or about the needs of our culture at a particular point in time, but also about the development of American Modernism in poetry? As the questions proliferated, I turned to Pound, choosing to focus on what I consider his most beautiful, integrated, and wise Cantos—the *Pisan Cantos*—which came late in his life and which, like Williams' *Paterson V,* were written at a time of intense crisis. And lastly, I turned to Eliot and his *Four Quartets,* his last poem, which seemed to me to share many of the qualities of these other long meditative poems. What did it mean that Eliot's poem came first? Did it in any way provide a model for the others? Or for Eliot himself?

The resulting book is not a systematic study of all the late poems of these poets. Rather I have chosen to concentrate in each case on one long poem, placing it in the context of earlier work. It is my hope that this book casts light on both an aging Modernism and the poetry of age (here I use the term "age" instead of "old age" for several reasons, one of which is simply that as I grew older in the course of this research, my notion of what is "old" changed, receding further into the future).

I have rehearsed at some length the path I took in choosing the poets included here because I want to emphasize that I did not begin my work with questions about the "images" of poets in their old age. If I had, I might have begun with Yeats, whose late poems are splendid and basically different in tone, as Daniel Albright shows in his book on

Yeats's poetry in old age:[1] like Dylan Thomas, Yeats rages against age, whereas, for the most part (this must be strictly qualified), these four American poets do not. And if I had, I might have written a book dominated by images of aging that would have sought, consciously, to champion the rights of the elderly as a dispossessed group, much as books have been written on behalf of women and their literature, blacks and their literature. I share that concern but it was not my initial purpose. As I have said, among other things, I was interested in understanding just what constitutes the style of the late poems of American Modernism, and thus this book invites further research along this line. To my mind, Eliot, Pound, Stevens, and Williams are our central Modern poets. But what about the late poems of Marianne Moore? Do they resemble the poems of these poets? And what of the poets who came after? Theodore Roethke's long meditative poems of the fifties?[2] Robert Duncan's poetry? Or Allen Ginsberg's recent poetry concerned with old age? I hope others will pursue these questions.

Nor did I undertake my research with a clear hypothesis about aging and the life cycle in mind, although in the process of research and writing, this book has no doubt acquired a polemical character. Generally speaking, there is nothing wrong with adopting a position on matters involving cultural choices, values, and practices; indeed, there is everything right in doing so, and this all too rarely happens in academic research. But in this case—research in the relatively new field of aging (especially new in literary studies)—there is a particular pitfall to be avoided, if possible.

The problem, or weakness, of research on aging and the elderly is that it tends to fall too easily into one of two overly simplified categories: either aging and old age are romanticized or they are presented as tragic twentieth-century injustices that can be alleviated, perhaps even rectified, through medical research and political and social reform. The literature of gerontology is characterized by bipolarity: unfortunately it tends to be either flatly optimistic or pessimistic. If Simone de Beauvoir's *The Coming of Age* and Robert Butler's *Why Survive: Being Old in America* tend toward the latter, my book tends toward the former. It does so, however, with the understanding basic to the humanities that I am concerned with the unique—in this case, with gifted writers—not a carefully selected cross-section of the population. This book, in other words, does not deal directly with the relationship between social problems and the literary mind, although it does imply that there are subtle connections between the larger needs of a culture and the artistic imagination. The focus is not on our stereotyped images of aging, which can indeed be uncovered through the study of literary texts, informing us about our blunt, often unseen cultural prejudices: I would hope my approach is more delicate than that.

If there is one discipline outside of literature that comes close to the approach of this book, it is developmental psychology, not social gerontology. One of the central conclusions of this book, for example, is that a new way of thinking (and thus being in the world), a new mode of cognition, may emerge in old age. Other areas of fruitful research in developmental psychology, not explored in this book, are suggested by its findings. I will cite just one example. David Levinson's research on adult development[3] reveals that a mentor—an older person who represents authority, a teacher, a sponsor, or a guide—is crucial to the years of early adulthood; the role of the mentor is to aid in the realization of one's dreams in life, which ultimately will require the rejection of the mentor. In the poems which I have studied closely— poems concerned with aging and old age instead of young adulthood—a wise figure also appears, but there is no implication that he must be discarded. Is this a developmental phenomenon? I would like to see research done on this question by developmental psychologists as well as scholars in the humanities.

Finally I should add that this book goes against the grain of much contemporary literary criticism, which is preoccupied with beginnings, the continual invention of the self, and the denial of origins. Edward Said, in his book *Beginnings,* writes that "paradoxically, an interest in beginnings is often the corollary of not believing that any beginning can be located."[4] This is not the case with endings. They can be located, tragically so, in a life, in a civilization. And they are too often denied. It may be characteristically American to see things in terms of beginnings, but I think it wise to shift our gaze to endings. Certainly it is sobering. For as Stevens wrote, so perfectly, in "Waving Adieu,

Adieu, Adieu,'' "In a world without heaven to follow, the stops/ Would be endings, more poignant than partings, profounder. . . ." And if a history of American poetics could be written in terms of our changing sense of beginnings, as Joseph Riddel proposes,[5] we must also begin to think of that history as having endings, and write that history as well.

I am deeply indebted to Roy Harvey Pearce, whom I hold dear as a mentor, and to the late Michel Benamou, whom I loved. I am grateful to Edwin Fussell, Joseph Riddel, Avrum Stroll, Andrew Wright, and Donald Wesling for their advice and encouragement. I am also grateful to Richard Rose for his perceptive and meticulous work in editing this book. I would like to thank the University of California at San Diego and the Department of English and the Center for Twentieth Century Studies at the University of Wisconsin-Milwaukee, especially Dean William Halloran, for their generous support of my research.

1. See Daniel Albright, *The Myth against Myth: A Study of Yeats's Imagination in Old Age* (London: Oxford University Press, 1972). His work shares many of the concerns of my own.

2. Ralph J. Mills, Jr., has done work on the late poems of Roethke. See his essay in *Cry of the Human: Essays in Contemporary American Poetry* (Urbana: University of Illinois Press, 1975).

3. David Levinson et al., *The Seasons of a Man's Life* (New York: Alfred A. Knopf, 1978).

4. Edward W. Said, *Beginnings: Intention and Method* (New York: Basic Books, 1975), p. 5.

5. Joseph Riddel, *The Inverted Bell: Modernism and the Counterpoetics of William Carlos Williams* (Baton Rouge: Louisiana State University Press, 1974), p. 44.

at last,
The Real Distinguished Thing

1

INTRODUCTION

"It must be believed," wrote Emerson in an essay entitled "Old Age," "that there is a proportion between the designs of a man and the length of his life: there is a calendar of his years, so of his performances."[1] Emerson's theory is characteristically optimistic: he proposes a model of the relationship between creation and the life cycle, which he finds fruitful for reasons of both personal and cultural health. In our age, we are for the most part skeptical, however. But what doubt we have about Emerson's theory of a just measure between performance and age, we must limit to specific cases. Our minds move to examples to test the theory: Wordsworth (the received wisdom of literary history instructs us) lived much too long, Anne Sexton too tragically brief a time. In this book I am concerned with four of our greatest Modern American poets of the twentieth century. I focus on four meditative poems—T. S. Eliot's *Four Quartets* (1943), Ezra Pound's *Pisan Cantos* (1948), "To an Old Philosopher in Rome" from Wallace Stevens' *The Rock* (1954), and the fifth book of *Paterson* (1958) by William Carlos Williams—considering each in the general context of the poet's poetry and prose, and in particular, his social thought. My purpose is not so much to test the theory as to point to our culture's need for the possibility it offers. For these poets, did aging and old age bring poetic fulfillment? Do these poets offer us insight into the experience of aging and its satisfactions?

The appropriate place to begin is with T. S. Eliot, whose work, reviewed briefly, can provide us with the historical *poetic* context in which to place these late Modern American poems. In 1915 Eliot introduced the world to "The Love Song of J. Alfred Prufrock," and in that portrait of a middle-aged man whose life is one of endless indecision, Eliot anticipated the uncertainty and debilitation engendered by World War I. Prufrock was bored and exhausted, so worn out in fact that by 1920 he had aged to become Gerontion, a shrunken man living in a rented house with nothing but his own tired thoughts to keep him company. Thirty-two years old at the time of the publication of "Gerontion," Eliot describes him as a little old man whose physical decrepitude is matched by the sterility of his meditations, "a dull head among windy spaces" who, having lost his "sight, smell, hearing, taste, and touch," is capable only of "thoughts of a dry brain in a dry season."[2] Then, as if it were not enough to personify the times in these portraits of Prufrock and Gerontion, two years later Eliot created a new poetic model, "The Waste Land," which itself expressed the fragmentation and sterility of the modern secular world, a culture that had no informing symbols, only a "heap of broken images." Together these three central poems—"Prufrock," "Gerontion," and "The Waste Land"—launched what has come to be known as the Age of Eliot.

But if the Age of Eliot began in exhaustion, it ended in affirmation. Eliot, and with him, Pound, Stevens, and Williams, confronted the collapse of order, and in their late poems, sought to discover, or generate, a new order, a new ground of authority. It is thus nonsense to conclude, as does a critic of Wallace Stevens, that "American poets have not, in general, aged well, because they have been unable to live their agedness with any fulness of being."[3] On the contrary, while most of the English Romantics, for example, burnt themselves out when they were young, these American poets reached into old age with intellectual vigor and poetic force. Pound was sixty-three when the *Pisan Cantos* were published, and both Stevens and Williams were seventy-five when their last books appeared. Eliot is an exception. His seventies were not poetically fertile; the *Four Quartets* was published when he was only in his fifties, but its voice and theme are definitely that of an older man. In these poems one impulse dominates individual variations: we do not find odes of dejection or the dusty thoughts of a Gerontion but poetic energy sustained by deep thought. These poets are our ancestors, men of exceptional intelligence and creativity who lived a long time, and as poets they must be lived with for a long time. And we owe it to ourselves to listen openly, for, as Eliot wrote, "you don't really criticize any author to whom you have never surrendered yourself.''[4]

In the *Four Quartets*, Eliot proposes a poetic point of unity, reestablishes the principle of authority on religious and literary grounds, and in so doing opens what we could call Late Modernism, that span of fifteen years dating from the publication of the *Four Quartets* in 1943 to the appearance of *Paterson V* in 1958. During these years American Modern poetry returns to the tradition of Romanticism (had it ever really left it?). Edwin Arlington Robinson's pronouncement of the death of great American poetry was much too premature: before the nineteenth century had even come to an end, he lamented that "the master songs are ended,'' because Whitman's poetry was "too powerfully pure,/too lovingly triumphant, and too large''[5] for a new age. But in the late work of Eliot, Pound, Stevens, and Williams, we have master songs of the twentieth century, and they are superb achievements, large, certainly, if not triumphantly expansive.

But the books are bound together by more than an affirmative vision.[6] Again it could be said that Eliot takes the lead and provides a model. The *Four Quartets* differs from "The Waste Land'' not only in its final effort at resolution, but also in its personalism, meditative mode, and more pronounced lyric clarity. And in general, these characteristics also appear in the late work of the other poets. We no longer encounter the careful impersonality of the poet that was the hallmark of much early American Modernism. Nor do we find the irony that imposes distance. Instead there is a new closeness, a more open dialogue between the poet and himself and between the poet and the reader. The Modern poet is no longer invisible. He shows us himself. The *Four Quartets*, the *Pisan Cantos*, *The Rock*, *Paterson V*—all represent the culmination of long poetic careers (although Pound did continue to write for many years), and all strive for transcendence of historical time, seeing history, as Eliot does in "Little Gidding,'' as "a pattern/Of timeless moments.''[7] In these poems the confusion of the urban collage of "The Waste Land'' is resolved, if only tentatively, in the central image of the sanctuary, partly religious, partly ironic, partly paradoxical, of a small enclosed space.

These poems are marked by a solitude of the self. The first four books of Williams' ambitious epic are dominated by the landscape of an industrial New Jersey city, with its polluted rivers and jammed elevators. The last book, written after the stroke that compelled him to abandon his medical practice, is pervaded by the religious quiet of the Cloisters in New York. Age forced a kind of disengagement[8] upon Williams that was totally new for him, and the remedy he sought was equally unparalleled in his past life—the acceptance of the European tradition, the shelter of the museum. For Pound, the humiliating, stifling U.S. prison camp in Pisa, Italy, where he was incarcerated in his sixties, yielded, paradoxically, a kind of grace. In Stevens' "To an Old Philosopher in Rome," the broad expanse of the West contracts to the silence of a small convent room. And in the last of Eliot's Quartets, "the light fails/... in a secluded chapel" in Little Gidding.

The quality of this silence is not empty and hollow, as is the Postmodern silence of Krapp's sputtering last tape in Samuel Beckett's play. It is orphic and sacramental, the source of language, the kind of silence that lets in symbolism, as the raucous neoromantic Norman O. Brown has put it.[9] Or as Eliot wrote in his moving essay on Goethe, "The wisdom of a human being resides as much in silence as in speech."[10] With the lessening of mobility imposed by age, space in these poems shrinks and disengagement from the social sphere takes place. But through the imagination, memory, and the meditative mode, this solitude brings new insights.

Each poet moved in his own way toward a kind of closure to his life in poetry. The poems are of course very different from one another. But as a group, they are characterized by (1) the central image of "the still point"; (2) a method of reflection, a new meditative mode, that denies the longheld Cartesian view of the act of the mind as conscious, voluntary, Promethean, and dominating, and stresses instead an easy penetration of mind and world, an ecology of mind; (3) a new hero, the wise old man, in a society that worships youth; and (4) a dedication to tradition and the creative act as a stay against chaos, and the life review. Thus, considered together, these four late works reveal a new development in lyric poetry that marks the last phase of American Modernism.

I. THE STILL POINT

In these late poems the past and tradition are not rejected but are recreated, and from what Eliot had called the wasteland emerges a new image that is potent and integrative, or at least signals the desire for such a symbol, a belief in its possibility. In "Burnt Norton," it is the "still point":

> At the still point of the turning world. Neither
> flesh nor fleshless;
> Neither from nor towards; at the still point,
> there the dance is,
> But neither arrest nor movement. And do not call
> it fixity,
> Where past and future are gathered. Neither
> movement from nor towards,
> Neither ascent nor decline. Except for the point,
> the still point,
> There would be no dance, and there is only the
> dance.

The desire is for wholeness, for a reconciliation of opposites ("Neither flesh nor fleshless; / Neither from nor towards"), for a state of being that is balanced at the source of change but not touched by it, for a moment of pure present-ness that can counteract the tyranny of biological and historical time without degenerating into stagnation ("do not call it fixity").

That point of stillness is the origin of meaningful creation, individual and cultural ("Except for the point, the still point, / There would be no dance"). It is a point of unity and deep peace, the point of eternal return, which is described as:

> The inner freedom from the practical desire,
> The release from action and suffering, release from the inner
> And the outer compulsion, yet surrounded
> By a grace of sense, a white light still and moving,
> *Erhebung* without motion, concentration
> Without elimination, both a new world

And the old made explicit, understood
In the completion of its partial ecstasy,
The resolution of its partial horror.

"Burnt Norton"

The still point is an image of a state of "grace," "still and moving."
Released from the demands of the world and inner pressures, one
stands outside of time and gains the perspective of wisdom ("both a
new world / And the old made explicit"). Thus it represents the ultimate goal of a person's life: enhanced spirituality, increased consciousness, and the inner peace that comes from an acceptance of the
"partial ecstasy" and "partial horror" of one's life and culture. The
hope, as Eliot puts it in the concluding lines of "Little Gidding," the
last of the *Four Quartets,* is that

We shall not cease from exploration
And the end of all our exploring
Will be to arrive where we started
And know the place for the first time.

One's life is a journey whose end has the power to illuminate one's
beginnings. One's end is a threshold where ideally "past and future are
gathered."

Eliot's still point is an ideal, a model of wholeness that was offered,
we might say, to Pound, Stevens, and Williams. The still point: its
equilibrium represents the simplest and most complete structure a system can assume under given conditions. It is a term that has entered the
vocabulary of the educated and can be sighted in such different fields
as ballet and the study of Zen.[11] It calls up the English Romantics who
were also preoccupied with the notion of the reconciliation of opposites. It is analogous to the "point suprême" of which Breton speaks.[12]
And it is described by Octavio Paz as the center of the Poem:

It is not impossible that, after this first and deceptive contact, the
reader may reach the center of the poem. Let us imagine that encounter.
In the flux and reflux of our passions and occupations (always divided,
always I and my double and the double of my other self), there is a
moment when everything comes to terms. The opposites do not disap-
pear, but are fused for an instant. It is a little like suspended animation:

time has no importance. The Upanishads teach that this reconciliation is *ananda* or bliss with the One. Of course, few are capable of reaching this state. But all of us, at some time, even for a fraction of a second, have glimpsed something similar. One does not have to be a mystic in order to know this truth.[13]

But above all, the still point refers to a means of articulating the relationship of the self to the world. For these four poets it is both different and the same. For Ezra Pound in the *Pisan Cantos* the still point is (among other things) the intersection of history and myth, the city "in the mind indestructible."[14] It may surprise us that a man who devoted so much of his energy to preserving objects and fragments of objects—a few lines of Sappho and the stone mermaids of Santa Maria Dei Miracoli—should understand the still point as a state of mind rather than the reconciliation of opposites embedded in artifact.

The reverse is true of William Carlos Williams. For him, in the fifth book of *Paterson,* the still point is to be found in the triumph of art over time and mortality. It is the museum made real, and here the still point refers not so much to a union of the self with the world as a strategy for escaping the world:

> It is the imagination
> which cannot be fathomed.
> It is through this hole
> we escape   .   .[15]

In the work of Wallace Stevens, on the other hand, the still point is not embodied, given body. It is neither sought in the medieval tapestries of the Cloisters, as it is in Williams, nor in a psychological/mystical state, as it is in Pound. For Stevens the still point is eternally elusive, a fiction ultimately abstract and metapoetic, the form to which concrete texts aspire. It is, as he puts it, the primitive like an orb, "the essential poem" that is found "at the centre of things." As he writes, wistfully, in "The Ultimate Poem Is Abstract":

> It would be enough
> If we were ever, just once, at the middle, fixed
> In This Beautiful World Of Ours and not as now,

> Helplessly at the edge, enough to be
> Completely, because at the middle, if only in sense,
> And in that enormous sense, merely enjoy.[16]

And for Eliot, who wished always to see the world through the filter of consciousness, who always was concerned with historical context, with growth, change, and decay, the still point is identified with knowledge and the redemption knowledge can bring, but is ultimately unattainable.

II. A NEW MEDITATIVE MODE

Late Modernism witnessed developments not only in poetry but also in the fields of anthropology and psychology which reveal an interest in wholeness and integration. As the intellectual historian Merle Curti observes, "In the later 1940s and throughout the 1950s the age-old quest for absolutes was pursued with fresh zest," and the answer given, he says, was essentially a religious or humanist one.[17] Thus on the one hand, Erich Neumann and Erik Erikson (the former a Jungian and the latter a neo-Freudian) proposed theories of psychological development and maturation that offer models for what Jung has called "centroversion," the achievement of psychic wholeness in the last phase of life. And on the other hand, the anthropologists Gregory Bateson and Victor Turner looked at the West from both within and without and concluded that we must adopt an ecological theory of mind, a systemic view of social change. What this suggests is that the common concerns of these psychologists and social scientists over the last thirty years have been anticipated, or paralleled, by the poets.

For Gregory Bateson, a work of art is fundamentally a quest for grace.[18] Although he writes about "primitive" visual art, we can apply his observations to the self-conscious poetry of the twentieth-century West as well. Certainly the connotations of the word "grace"—religious favor, prayer, compassion, good fortune, the unerring beauty of poise, the Greek goddesses, moral virtue—capture some of the concerns and qualities of these late poems of Eliot, Pound, Stevens, and Williams. But for Bateson grace is ultimately something more abstract. It is essentially a problem of integrating the diverse parts of the mind, and this integration exists on not just an individual level but a cultural level as well. Every culture, he concludes, has a characteristic species of grace toward which it is striving, and this can be read in its art. The terms that he uses to describe this integration are essentially Jungian: art delivers "a message about the interface between conscious and unconscious."[19] Rather than holding to the Freudian notion of art as symptom, Bateson believes that art *speaks* a *hidden* truth; it does not hide a truth.

Taken together, these American poems share a conclusive distrust of the conscious, muscular, Promethean act of the mind. They signal a return to tradition, to metaphor, and to a reliance on the creative readiness that can yield the epiphanic moment. In this way the history of American Modernism fulfills Bateson's notion of the more specific role art has to play today if we are to extricate ourselves from the nightmare of our technological civilization. For art, he believes, calls attention to an ecological view of life which compensates for our *too-purposive* Western view of life. This is the wisdom that art can impart. "Wisdom," he writes, "I take to be the knowledge of the larger interactive system—that system which if disturbed, is likely to generate exponential curves of change."[20] Humility is a part of this wisdom, the knowledge that man is only part of a larger system and that the part can never ultimately control the whole. This is the humility that the American Moderns call for, either explicitly or implicitly.

Perhaps more importantly, this humility is also dramatized by the mode of these meditative poems. It is possible, Bateson believes, that the cure for the excesses of conscious purpose lies first with the individual rather than with the wholesale reform of institutions. In art, dreams, and religion the whole person is involved and "must necessarily relax that arrogance [of the conscious mind] in favor of a creative experience in which his conscious mind plays only a small part." He concludes that "in creative art man must experience himself—his total self—as a cybernetic model."[21] At its best, in other words, the meditative mode of these late poems operates on a new principle of selecting "information." It provides us with a model of correct thought, just as the nineteenth-century Romantic landscape poem did in its time. The meditative mode is thus a way of uniting the self and the world through the agency of the mind, but we must not make the mistake of understanding mind as being limited to only conscious mind.

Here the model of mind described by Bateson converges with that of the psychologist Erik Erikson. The wisdom of the meditative mode parallels the strength of what Erikson calls the eighth and final stage of psychosocial development of the life cycle. The decisive choice in this stage of old age, Erikson hypothesizes, is between the attitudes of integrity and despair:

> *Wisdom, then is detached concern with life itself, in the face of death itself.* It maintains and conveys the integrity of experience. . . . If vigor of mind combines with the gift of responsible renunciation, some old people can envisage human problems in their entirety (which is what "integrity" means) and can represent to the coming generation a living example of the "closure" of a style of life. Only such integrity can balance the despair of the knowledge that a limited life is coming to a conscious conclusion.[22]

Strength thus inheres in being able to continue with dignity, *to be,* while facing the reality of *not being.*

Erikson's phrase *"detached concern"* provides us with a key to understanding the process of achieving this state of mind, this state of grace: the meditative mode requires not so much an *act* of the mind as a *state of receptivity* to experience. In this final stage of life, unity is not discovered by the arduous, formulaic jesuitical meditation Loyola recommended: composition, discourse, and colloquy.[23] The kind of thinking involved is not category-making and abstraction. The goal is to *discover* rather than to impose or to reason.

How is the meditative mode described by the poets? It occurs, Eliot wrote, "at rare moments of inattention and detachment, drowsing in sunlight."[24] The illumination of the "unexpected moment" appears when one is not consciously, purposively, looking for it. The meditative mode of these poems of old age is Heideggerian. It is characterized by a quiet openness to the primal realities of human experience which allows them simply *to be,* to disclose themselves before the gaze of the whole mind. Here we might speculate, as scholars in other disciplines are doing, to what extent this kind of "thinking" characterizes, either totally or partially, a last stage of life—senectitude. With the contraction of space, the imposition of physical immobility, and the condition of solitude, perhaps a new mode of cognition develops that is satisfying and non-Promethean.[25]

III. THE WISE OLD MAN AS HERO

In these poems a new image of nobility and authority appears: the figure of the wise old man as hero. This is significant because so much has been said about the adolescent hero in our literature and the frenetic cult of youth in America. But it is a corrective we needed and still need. The tradition of the new, still rampant, requires its opposite, the wisdom of the tradition of the old made new. If we can read the shape of history from literature, then in the forties and fifties we desired a new form of heroism, or at least, a new sense of tradition and continuity to counter a throw-away culture. For the abundance of America can no longer be thought of in terms of increasing consumer indexes. The people of a once-expanding land of plenty must reconceive space in interior terms. It is clearly no longer appropriate, nor correct, to apostrophize the United States, as Whitman did, as the greatest poem.

But the compensation could be this: in these four Moderns we see that the American Adam has grown up, and more importantly, he has grown old with grace and dignity. Whereas "Gerontion" is a "dull head among windy spaces," in these poems the supreme humanist symbol is transformed from the primitive orb of the poem (a fiction) into the wise old man (a reality) in search of what will suffice. Eliot had written prophetically in "East Coker" that "Old men ought to be explorers." And, in fact, in these late poems it is often the very presence of a teacher, an embodiment of tradition and continuity, that is sought. Stevens' Santayana and Eliot's composite figure of his literary ancestors (the ghost), Pound's Confucius and Williams' Toulouse-Lautrec, to whom he dedicates *Paterson V*—all represent not only tradition but are also *doppelgängers,* secret selves.

For at its best a literary symbol, in addition to its historical context, has a personal dimension that acts to transform the self. Thus we understand how important these master figures are for the poets and, in turn, how important for us are these aging poets: they have given us images of balance achieved only after a long life of reflection and creative work. As Theodore Roszak writes in *Where the Wasteland Ends,* "A true symbol must be *lived into,* that is how its meaning is found."[26] Our culture must absorb these poems into the body politic and thereby take the words to heart.

We can also look at this from a slightly different point of view. "Achieving the impossible," Robert Nisbet writes, "is what metaphor is all about. From it springs religions, prophecies, and dogmas."[27] If the image of the still point, which unites these poems of maturity and old age, is indeed the *root metaphor* of American Modern poetry (and the wasteland is not), and if a root metaphor expresses what cannot yet be expressed as conscious thought, poetry is indeed prophecy or at least the voicing of need, of desire.[28] In what sense, then, are these poets our prophets? What is their legacy?

As Erikson has said, "A civilization can be measured by the meaning which it gives to the full cycle of life, for such meaning, or the lack of it, cannot fail to reach into the beginnings of the next generation, and thus into the chances of others to meet ultimate questions with some clarity and strength."[29] In the West, the aged are devalued in direct proportion to their loss of power, which is measured in economic terms. This view of the aged signals disaster for our civilization, for human dignity is denied, continuity broken, the cohesion of community destroyed. Simone de Beauvoir makes the same point. In *La Vieillesse,* which her American publisher issued under the misleading and euphemistic title *The Coming of Age,* she writes, in words that recall those of Erikson, "the meaning or lack of meaning that old age takes on in any given society puts that whole society to the test, since it is this that reveals the meaning or lack of meaning of the entirety of life leading to that old age."[30] She urges us to concentrate our efforts on the most oppressed of our elderly. But we must look also at those who provide models of the fullest possibility. This would involve us in the relationship between creativity and old age, an area that up until now has been largely ignored.[31]

The figure of the heroic wise old man we must not overly idealize however. Serenity is not undisturbed; balance is not easily won or preserved. In the *Pisan Cantos,* for example, Pound is cranky as well as benevolently wise. Eliot's voice is wise, but his vision of old age is basically grim. Williams exhorts Paterson (himself) to "keep your pecker up / whatever the detail!" (V,iii).

And the tone of *The Rock,* although ever well-measured, is alternately one of a balanced tranquility, delight, and a weary sadness; in taking stock of his life and his work, Stevens acknowledges a sense of failure as well as newfound pleasures and ways of being. On the whole, then, for these four poets, the condition of integrity, to use Erikson's term, achieved in, or imagined for, old age is no simple state of being. Above all, perhaps, it is characterized by humility (and this returns us to the meditative mode) that contradicts the Western way of thinking about mankind in the world—imperialism over nature and other peoples. Old age brings an end to domination. Man stripped of such physical, perhaps overbearing, strength is what Stevens imagines in "Lebensweisheitspielerei," which I quote here in full:

> Weaker and weaker, the sunlight falls
> In the afternoon. The proud and the strong
> Have departed.
>
> Those that are left are the unaccomplished,
> The finally human,
> Natives of a dwindled sphere.
> Their indigence is an indigence
> That is an indigence of the light,
> A stellar pallor that hangs on the threads.
> Little by little, the poverty
> Of autumnal space becomes
> A look, a few words spoken.
>
> Each person completely touches us
> With what he is and as he is,
> In the stale grandeur of annihilation.

It is "the finally human" which "touches us," a deepening of the human spirit made possible in and by old age.

IV. TRADITION, CREATION, AND THE LIFE REVIEW

Of the four poets Pound was submitted to the most severe physical, psychological, and social pressure in his old age, both in the Italian prison camp and later in Washington at St. Elizabeth's. He had to start again, to find not only what could "suffice," in Wallace Stevens' cool term, but what he could live on. After all he was branded a traitor (understandably since he had spoken in favor of the enemy), his betrayal a result of believing in the wrong values at the wrong time in the wrong place. His solution would be a return to the past, not a projection into the future.

What he could live on was, in part, the memory of both people and places, art works and historical events and monuments. Robert Butler has suggested that the predominance of the shades of memory in the elderly is not necessarily a sign of senility or psychological imbalance, but may very well be a functional mechanism by which man comes to terms with his past life.[32] Certainly this is the case for Pound. He asserts "Senesco sed amo" (LXXX), which is both a personal revelation and a declaration as to how to live. He literally plots the curve of his own past, just as Eliot provides us in the *Four Quartets* with a model for that plot:

> . . . the end of all our exploring
> Will be to arrive where we started
> And know the place for the first time.

But we must remark that Pound's "past" extends beyond his own life to the troubadours of the twelfth century, the literature of Greece and Rome, and African myth.

Perhaps just as significant (and this is a kind of lesson in the politics of the elderly), one of the primary catalysts in transforming his life in prison into magical moments of paradise, is his acknowledging brotherhood with other prisoners—criminals—of the camp. Paradoxically the forced space and forced time provided him, although against his will, the freedom for a life review. Thus in the *Pisan Cantos* Pound moves beyond the elite sphere of history, literature, and myth and into the world of outcast men. He magnificently unites the two, learning much, remaking himself, and creating one of his finest poems.

The work of the anthropologist Victor Turner can help us understand, I think, both how Pound was "made new" and how the elderly today form a key sector along the frontier of cultural adaptation.[33] In *Dramas, Fields, and Metaphors*,[34] Turner discusses our fundamental need for what he calls "communitas," a condition of social unity (community) characterized by undifferentiated social status (what Martin Buber has termed the "I-Thou" relationship of the self to the other) and a time that is not socio-historical time but sacred time. Above all, communitas is not merely metaphorical; it is a relationship between concrete individuals (the pilgrimage is an excellent example of communitas).

To communitas Turner opposes "structure," by which he means the hierarchal, stratified, bureaucratic structure we encounter in the institutions of the family, the orthodox church, the corporation, and so on. The dialectic of the two poles of communitas and structure, Turner argues, is a useful conceptual tool for understanding the process of social change, that includes the revitalization of institutions, the replacement of one institution by another, and so on. It is communitas that is the condition "for the production of root metaphors, conceptual archetypes, paradigms, models" and that thus provides the impetus for significant social change.[35] Of the four poets, it is only Pound who succeeds in clearly dramatizing this need for community and suggesting what power the condition of communitas has. In the prison camp of Pisa, he and the other prisoners are divested of all status, as are the elderly in our society, and from their mutual bondage, a close social bond is formed.

If an image of this social bond among marginals was not possible for Eliot, or Stevens, or Williams, certainly for all of them (although here we might question Stevens), the gift of history and tradition is a partial answer to the anguish of old age and death. In these poems, the past is recovered and placed in the present, itself renewed, a renewing force. The thrust is a conservative one. To conserve and preserve one's origins, one's heritage, to expand one's cultural past so as to create new possibilities for the present and the future—that is the goal. The question is a political as well as a literary one, and of the four, Stevens is the only one who does not offer a solution, however small it might be, to the dehumanization and fragmentation of the Western industrial world.

In his essay on "Art and Time," the depth psychologist Erich Neumann uses the word "transcendent" to describe the quality that is found in the work of great artists in old age. In a creative solitude, such artists move beyond the limitation of their age, in both senses of the word. Neumann cites the self-portraits of the aged Rembrandt, the late paintings of Titian, the late plays of Shakespeare, and the late quartets of Beethoven. In these works, he says, we find "a strange figuration, a breakthrough into the realm of essences."[36] I quote Neumann at some length:

Tempest?

> In these works of man a numinous world is manifested in which the polarity of outward and inward—nature and art—seems to be resolved. Their secret alchemy achieves a synthesis of the numinosum at the heart of nature and psyche.
> These aged masters seem to have attained the image and likeness of a primal creative force, prior to the world and outside the world, which, though split from the very beginning into the polarity of nature and psyche, is in essence one divided whole.
>
> . . . .
>
> This art no longer relates either consciously or unconsciously to any historical time; the solitary monologue of these "extreme" works is spoken, as it were, into the void. And one cannot quite tell whether it is a monologue or a dialogue between man and the ultimate.
>
> . . . .
>
> But in the rare instances when the phenomenon of transcendence occurs, the transpersonal seems, even though it has passed through the medium of the human, to have achieved its own objectivity—to speak, one might say, with itself. It is no longer oriented toward the world or man, the ego or the collective, security or insecurity; instead, the creative act which mysteriously creates form and life in nature as in the human psyche seems to have perceived itself and to shine forth with its own incandescence. The creative impulse seems to have liberated itself. United on the plane of artistic-creation, the self which man experiences within him and the world-creative self which is manifested outwardly achieve the transparency of symbolic reality.[37]

Although I am not sure in what way historical realities are ever transcended in a work of art, I do understand, and accept, what Neumann points to. The poems of Stevens, Eliot, Pound, and Williams do possess an orphic quality, a timeless dimension, which links them with what can only be called the age-old wisdom of humanity.

For Neumann, man is not a one-dimensional political or economic animal. Rather Neumann calls for a "mystical anthropology"; he is concerned with *homo mysticus,* with mysticism not limited to the experience of God but understood as a fundamental, broadly based category of human experience. Following Jung's model of individuation (the striving of the individual toward psychic wholeness), Neumann argues that different forms of mysticism accompany the three major stages of psychological development: we find source mysticism in the uroboros stage where the unconscious is dominant, hero mysticism in the second phase where the ego is dominant, and mature mysticism in the final stage where the self emerges: opposites are reconciled, and harmony is achieved between the conscious and unconscious aspects of the mind.

More specifically, the final stage of Old Age Neumann identifies with the mysticism of the Egyptian god Osiris and *The Tibetan Book of the Dead.* In this stage the self becomes transparent, he says; the world becomes transparent, and the mystical experience is a conscious one. The possibility of the symbolic life is revealed, and life in the world becomes possible, even in the face of death. Thus Neumann explores the archetype of the Wise Old Man through its manifestations in texts drawn from both literature and the visual arts, which are themselves the creations of men in old age. Literature, he finds, reveals the achievement of wisdom in our time and records the potentialities of human experience.

Jung's description of the archetype of the Wise Old Man not only accords with Neumann's findings (this is not surprising) but also corresponds to Erikson's notion of the final stage of a person's development in old age:

> In the encounter with life and the world there are experiences that are capable of moving us to long and thorough reflection, from which, in time, insights and convictions grow up—a process depicted by the alchemists as the philosophical tree. The unfolding of these experiences is regulated, as it were, by two archetypes: the anima, who expresses *life,* and the "Wise Old Man," who personifies *meaning. . . .* This aptly describes the character of that spirit or thinking which you do not, like an intellectual operation, perform yourself, as the "little god of this world," but which happens to you as though it came from another, and greater, perhaps the great spirit of the world. . . .[38]

The involuntary character of the archetype fits the description that the poets give of the meditative mode and the symbols that emerge from this state of being.

Perhaps the long life of the imagination compensates for the losses of the social world. Perhaps some form of mystical experience is possible. If so, it does not result from an "intellectual operation" that one performs like a "god." It simply happens, and happens as the result of a long life of writing, a long life of working with images. All of this is metaphor for the creative process. Neumann describes it this way:

> It is characteristic of the creative process that in it the ego cannot cling to its position of consciousness, but must expose itself to encounter with the nonego. In so doing, the ego renounces conscious reality in which the world is experienced as contradiction, and an encounter occurs between ego and nonego in which the contradictions of the world, ego, and self are suspended. This encounter, wherever it may occur, we designate as mystical.[39]

This is the still point, with the reconciliation of opposites being described in psychoanalytical terms. The mature phase of old age can be understood as a new synthesis between the conscious ego and the nonego, an integration of the personality with the self, not the ego, at the center.

What these depth psychologists describe as an archetypal process, what Erikson and Neumann have to say about the final stage in man's development, is clearly pertinent to the study of the late poems of these American poets. This will be offensive to many who find these notions soft, romantic, and mushy-minded. I agree we must be careful. And this brings me to the theme with which I opened this chapter—Emerson's theory of a just proportion between age and creation. For the truth value of the constructions of developmental psychology is not at stake here. Nor would I argue that these poems are expressions of universal values and thus transcend their culture. Although theories of the evolution of personal consciousness play a backstage part in reading the late poems of these Modern poets, it is not the case that the theory predicts the poems or that the poems verify the theory. Nor is this the sheltered circularity of an argument that can only reproduce itself, a flat tautology.

One does not, in other words, have to *apply* psychological analysis to poetry. Nor should one. When a paradigm pervades an age, it offers models of thinking that are explicit in scientific thought but remain implicit in poetic practice. For the imagination does not argue, as James Hillman has said, *it imagines*.[40] And thus what we read in the poets and psychologists is an expression of the collective imagination of the Modern American Age. Both reflect the needs and beliefs of a cultural period. The work of the poets corroborates the findings of these developmental psychologists. And in turn, the work of the latter illuminates the visions of the Modern poets. They each give assent to the other. And they do so precisely because they hold the same all-pervading assumptions about the possibility of holistic integrations of individual lives for the survival of men and mankind. Thus, the two modes of inquiry—that of the poet and that of the psychologist—reinforce each other and in so doing help us understand the spirit and values of an age. Basically, both the humanistic psychology of Erikson and Neumann, Jung and Schachtel,[41] and the poems of these four poets propose a model of growth that applies to personal and cultural development (there are exceptions, of course, as we will see). It is this assumption that gives body to their theories and generates their poems, a romantic belief that embodies the hope of the Modern age, a belief that must both be taken seriously and questioned.

In general, then, these are the common grounds that invite comparison of the *Four Quartets,* the *Pisan Cantos, The Rock,* and *Paterson V.* But to the literary mind, differences are more important than similarities, and each of these books offers a unique solution (if I may use that word) to a particular problem. Thus each book, and each poet, demands its own approach. Although in the four essays that follow comparison is the chief rationale for bringing these poems together and remains the central method for judging them (I assume that the readers are familiar with these poems and thus make comparisons among the poets and their poems within the chapters), the convergence of models—both among the models themselves and with the poems—cannot, should not, blind us to the individualities of each. This was the criterion to which I eventually submitted my work. In spite of likenesses, would the differences survive critical attention? I hope so, for significant information is difference that makes a difference, and these books present four converging but separate visions of aging, old age, and an aging Modernism.

1. Ralph Waldo Emerson, *Society and Solitude* (Boston: Fields, Osgood & Co., 1870), p. 296.

2. T. S. Eliot, *The Waste Land and Other Poems* (New York: Harcourt, Brace, & World, 1962), pp. 19–22.

3. Merle E. Brown, *Wallace Stevens: The Poem as Act* (Detroit: Wayne State University Press, 1970), p. 175.

4. Quoted in Stephen Spender, "Remembering Eliot," in *T. S. Eliot: The Man and His Work,* ed. Allen Tate (New York: Dell, 1966), p. 55.

5. E. A. Robinson, "Walt Whitman," in *The Children of the Night* (New York: Macmillan, 1921).

6. These Modern meditative poems resemble what M. H. Abrams has called "the greater romantic lyric" ("Structure and Style in the Greater Romantic Lyric," in *From Sensibility to Romanticism: Essays Presented to Frederick A. Pottle,* ed. Frederick W. Hilles and Harold Bloom [New York: Oxford University Press, 1965], pp. 527–58.) In an admirable essay, Abrams describes the genre to which such poems as Wordworth's "Tintern Abbey," Coleridge's "Frost at Midnight" and "Dejection: An Ode," and Keats' "Ode to a Nightingale" belong: "Some of the poems are called odes, while the others approach the ode in having lyric magnitude and a serious subject, feeling fully meditated. They present a determinate speaker in a particularized, and usually a localized, outdoor setting, whom we overhear as he carries on, in a fluent vernacular which rises easily to a more formal speech, a sustained colloquy, sometimes with himself or with the outer scene, but more frequently with a silent human auditor, present or absent. The speaker begins with a description of the landscape; an aspect or change of aspect in the landscape evokes a varied but integral process of memory, thought, anticipation, and feeling which remains closely intervolved with the outer scene. In the course of this meditation the lyric speaker achieves an insight, faces up to a tragic loss, comes to a moral decision, or resolves an emotional problem. Often the poem rounds upon itself to end where it began, at the outer scene, but with an altered mood and deepened understanding which is the result of the intervening meditation." There are three major differences between what I am calling the Modern meditative poem and the nineteenth-century Romantic lyric, however. First, Abrams notes a similarity between the meditative structure of the greater Romantic lyric and that of the seventeenth-century devotional poem as it has been described by Louis Martz in his splendid study *The Poetry of Meditation* (New Haven: Yale University Press, 1954); I stress the *dis*similarity between the meditative mode of the late Modern American poem and that of St. Ignatius of Loyola, and enlarge upon this question later in this chapter. Second, Abrams points out that the greater Romantic lyric often is characterized by a mood of dejection and profound sadness; the American poem, on the contrary, although concerned with crisis, is basically characterized by a

sense of resolution. And third, the Romantic lyric displays an interest in landscape that is not shared (with the exception of Pound's *Pisan Cantos*) by its descendant.

7. T. S. Eliot, *Four Quartets* (New York: Harcourt, Brace, 1943). All references will be to this edition and will be identified by the name of the Quartet only.

8. I use the word "disengagement" advisedly. Social gerontology has long been dominated by two competing theories of successful aging—the activity theory and the disengagement theory. In its *classic* form, the disengagement theory argues that the withdrawal of the individual from active social roles is a mutually satisfying process for both the individual and the society. Functionalist in approach, the theory maintains that through disengagement, society prepares for the disruption in the social fabric that death inevitably brings, and the individual readies himself for the personal crisis of death. Disengagement, it is hypothesized, is a universal phenomenon, not a practice cultivated only by certain cultures. Accordingly, the theory of disengagement proposes that old age is a distinct phase in the psychosocial development of the individual and that the process promotes the health of a culture as well as the spiritual realization of the individual (see Elaine Cumming and William Henry, *Growing Old: The Process of Disengagement* [New York: Basic Books, 1961]). Disengagement from the social world need not of course entail disengagement from the imaginative world of writing. In the late poems of Eliot, Pound, Stevens, and Williams, however, it should be noted that social disengagement, whether chosen or forced, offers satisfactions as well as pain. On the whole, disengagement from an active social world is not negative. I realize, of course, that writing is also a social activity, particularly in the case of four esteemed, indeed lionized, poets. But nonetheless, the image presented of the solitary poet is, on balance, positive.

9. Norman O. Brown, *Love's Body* (New York: Random House, 1966), p. 190.

10. T. S. Eliot, "Goethe as the Sage," *On Poetry and Poets* (New York: Noonday Press, 1961), p. 257.

11. One of Tod Bolender's ballets is entitled "The Still Point" and so is William Johnson's book on Zen, which contains a good deal of discussion of Eliot's notion of the still point. See his *The Still Point: Reflections on Zen and Christian Mysticism* (New York: Harper and Row, 1970).

● 12. André Breton, "Second Manifesto of Surrealism," in *Manifestoes of Surrealism,* trans. Richard Seaver and Helen R. Lane (Ann Arbor: University of Michigan Press, 1969), pp. 123–24: "Everything tends to make us believe that there exists a certain point of the mind at which life and death, the real and the imagined, past and future, the communicable and the incommunicable, high and low, cease to be perceived as contradictions. Now, search as one may one will never find any other motivating force in the activities of the Surrealists than the hope of finding and fixing this point."

13. Octavio Paz, *The Bow and the Lyre,* trans. Ruth L. C. Simms (Austin: University of Texas Press, 1973), p. 14.

14. Ezra Pound, *The Cantos of Ezra Pound* (New York: New Directions, 1970), p. 430. All references will be to this edition and will be identified by the number of the Canto only.

15. William Carlos Williams, *Paterson* (New York: New Directions, 1963), V, i.

All references will be to this edition and will be identified by the title or number of the book and the section within that book only.

16. Wallace Stevens, "A Primitive Like an Orb," "The Ultimate Poem Is Abstract," *The Collected Poems of Wallace Stevens* (New York: Alfred A. Knopf, 1968). All references will be to this edition and will be identified by title only.

17. Merle Curti, *The Growth of American Thought,* 3rd ed. (New York: Harper and Row, 1964), p. 767.

18. Gregory Bateson, *Steps to an Ecology of Mind* (New York: Ballantine, 1972).

19. *Steps to an Ecology of Mind,* p. 138.

20. *Steps to an Ecology of Mind,* p. 433.

21. *Steps to an Ecology of Mind,* p. 438.

22. Erik Erikson, *Insight and Responsibility: Lectures on the Ethical Implications of Psychoanalytical Insight* (New York: W. W. Norton, 1964), pp. 133–34.

23. See Louis Martz, *The Poem of the Mind: Essays on Poetry/English and American* (New York: Oxford University Press, 1966) and *The Poetry of Meditation* for the opposite point of view. On the other hand, in *The Continuity of American Poetry* (Princeton: Princeton University Press, 1961), Roy Harvey Pearce has pointed out that for American poets the appropriate meditative model is Puritan, not Jesuitical: "For the Puritan (particularly the New England Puritan, who was much more conservative than his English peer) meditation, then, was a matter not of disciplining one's self into knowledge of God (which was impossible) but of being lucky enough to catch a sudden glimpse of that knowledge as God might make manifest" (p. 43).

24. T. S. Eliot, "John Marston," in *Elizabethan Essays* (New York: Haskell House, 1964), p. 194. Attracted to the description of the creative moment as occuring in the blurred locus of the worlds of sleep and consciousness, Eliot includes in *After Strange Gods* (London: Faber and Faber, 1934), p. 45, a passage from Yeats' essay on "The Symbolism of Poetry," which refers to this state of mind: "The purpose of rhythm, it has always seemed to me, is to prolong the moment of contemplation, the moment when we are both awake and asleep, which is the one moment of creation, by hushing us with an alluring monotony, while it holds us waking by its variety, to keep us in that state of perhaps real trance, in which the mind liberated from the pressure of the will is unfolded in symbols." Although Eliot comments that "there is a good deal of truth in this theory," but not enough (p. 45), he challenges not so much the poetic process as the overly fanciful, artificial symbols themselves (the dreamlike world of Fergus, and so forth) of Yeats' imagination.

25. See Stuart F. Spicker, "Gerontogenetic Mentation: Memory, Dementia, and Medicine in the Penultimate Years," in *Aging and the Elderly: Humanistic Perspectives in Gerontology,* ed. Stuart F. Spicker, Kathleen Woodward, and David D. Van Tassel (Atlantic Highlands, N.J.: Humanities Press, 1978), pp. 153–80. For a related discussion of aging and time from a philosophical point of view, see C. Davis Hendricks and Jon Hendricks, "Historical Development of the Multiplicity of Times and Implications for the Analysis of Aging," *The Human Context,* 7(1975), 117–29.

26. Theodore Roszak, *Where the Wasteland Ends: Politics and Transcendence in Post-Industrial Society* (Garden City, N.Y.: Doubleday, 1973), pp. 128–29.

27. Robert Nisbet, *Social Change and History: Aspects of the Western Theory of Development* (New York: Oxford University Press, 1969), p. 241.

28. Stephen C. Pepper calls the kind of metaphor that underlies and dominates an age (an example might be the seventeenth-century idea of society, man, and the universe as machinelike) a "root metaphor." See his *World Hypotheses* (Berkeley: University of California Press, 1942).

29. Erik Erikson, *Identity, Youth, and Crisis* (New York: W. W. Norton, 1968), pp. 140–41.

30. Simone de Beauvoir, *The Coming of Age,* trans. Patrick O'Brian (New York: Warner Paperback Library, 1973), p. 18.

31. See, for example, the pioneer issue of the *Journal of Geriatric Psychiatry,* 6(1973), which is devoted to "Psychoanalytic Concepts of Creativity and Aging."

32. Robert Butler, "The Life Review: An Interpretation of Reminiscence in the Aged," in *Middle Age and Aging: A Reader in Social Psychology,* ed. Bernice L. Neugarten (Chicago: University of Chicago Press, 1968), pp. 486–96.

33. Gerald Gruman makes this point. See his essay on the "Cultural Origins of Present-day 'Age-ism': The Modernization of the Life Cycle," in *Aging and the Elderly,* pp. 359–87.

34. Victor Turner, *Dramas, Fields, and Metaphors: Symbolic Action in Human Society* (Ithaca: Cornell University Press, 1974).

35. *Dramas, Fields, and Metaphors,* p. 38. Turner associates communitas with "liminality," a term he borrows from Van Gennep; liminality, referring to a threshold situation, a gap between one ordered world and another, is an excellent metaphor for these late poems.

36. Erich Neumann, *Art and the Creative Unconscious,* trans. Ralph Manheim (Princeton, N.J.: Princeton University Press, 1971), p. 103.

37. *Art and the Creative Unconscious,* pp. 103–5.

38. Carl Gustav Jung, *Mysterium Coniunctionis: An Inquiry into the Separation and Synthesis of Psychic Opposites in Alchemy,* trans. R. F. C. Hull, 2nd ed. (Princeton, N.J.: Princeton University Press, 1970), p. 233.

39. Erich Neumann, "Mystical Man" [1948], in *The Mystic Vision,* Bollingen Series XXX: Papers from the Eranos Yearbooks, Vol. 6, ed. Joseph Campbell (Princeton: Princeton University Press, 1969), pp. 375–415.

40. James Hillman, *Re-visioning Psychology* (New York: Harper and Row, 1975), p. 214.

41. Ernest G. Schachtel is less well known than the other psychologists mentioned here. See his *Metamorphosis: On the Development of Affect, Perception, Attention, and Memory* (New York: Basic Books, 1959).

2

T. S. ELIOT AND THE *FOUR QUARTETS*
The Still Point, Aging, and the Social Bond

After the kingfisher's wing
Has answered light to light, and is silent, the light is still
At the still point of the turning world.—"Burnt Norton"

Eliot would certainly have objected to the often-voiced view that in the still point of the *Four Quartets,* he had created a symbol, as though he had fashioned a planet and hurled it into the heavens. As we well know, Eliot wanted not to create but to discover. He was no system-builder in the manner of Yeats and Blake. "Man is man," he wrote in his 1928 essay entitled "Second Thoughts about Humanism," "because he can recognize supernatural realities, not because he can invent them."[1] Moreover, if we understand, as we should, that a symbol has an experiential dimension, that it is a magical object that works a transformation of the self, then we should not confer upon the still point the status of a symbol for Eliot. As Roszak explains: "True symbols transcend intellectual deciphering, calling forth another level of consciousness which eludes words. They are, as it were, doors leading into dark chambers of reality, like the entranceways of the old mystery cults. We must take our whole life in with us and be prepared to be totally transformed."[2] In Pound's *Pisan Cantos* we find this experiential dimension on all levels; in the *Four Quartets* we do not. In the still point Eliot has neither created a symbol for himself nor has he discovered a true magical object. But the irony is that he has *invented a term* which has life, which spoke to his generation and continues to speak to ours. The irony is that Stevens' notes never built a supreme fiction, but Eliot's still point functions as one.

The still point, then, is not a symbol but more like a definition. As Eliot wrote in his confident and clear-minded 1916 Harvard doctoral dissertation, which was published under the title *Knowledge and Experience in the Philosophy of F. H. Bradley*: "That at which we aim is the real as such; and the real as such is not an object. When we define an experience, we substitute the definition for the experience, and then experience the definition; though the original experience may have been itself a definition: but the experiencing is quite another thing from the defining.''[3]

The still point is a hybrid, let us call it a construction, part image and part concept,[4] the locus perhaps of the two in a modern world where geometry is skewed and parallel planes intersect. It is a fitting, in fact a brilliant, solution for a poet who owed much, perhaps against his will, to the symbolist aesthetic, and who believed, against the main current of twentieth-century Western thought, in the Christian world view.

I. VARIETIES OF RELIGIOUS AND LITERARY EXPERIENCE

Consequently I rejoice, having to construct something
Upon which to rejoice

"Ash Wednesday"[5]

To begin, we must distinguish between *the* still point and *a* still point, or more accurately, "the unattended moment." First, the still point is a model, an ideal construct, a point that does not and cannot exist within the normal human domain but instead represents a goal which man strives to both comprehend and attain. The still point, in other words, has a clear Christian referent. Unlike Blake, Eliot did not have to create philosophy as well as poetry. He believed in a traditional and coherent system of belief, or at least he believed it was necessary to believe. As he says somewhat pragmatically in his essay on Dante, the advantage to the poet (and to the reader) of having such a system at his disposal is that "it stands apart, for understanding and assent even without belief, from the single individual who propounds it.''[6] The still point belongs to such an encircling system of distinctly defined correspondences. It refers to both a state of mind, which is perfect Christian peace, and to the principle of Incarnation. It is miraculous and does not admit either skepticism or doubt:

The hint half guessed, the gift half understood, is Incarnation.
Here the impossible union

> Of spheres of existence is actual,
> Here the past and future
> Are conquered, and reconciled. . . .
>
> > "The Dry Salvages"

As such, the still point is _posited_ by Eliot as poet but not _experienced_ by Eliot as a character in the *Four Quartets.*

For Eliot, man's common, conscious state of mind is suffering and torment, and even to apprehend the Incarnation, to lay hold of its meaning as both event and principle, is a possibility only for saints:

> But to apprehend
> The point of intersection of the timeless
> With time, is an occupation for the saint—
> No occupation either, but something given
> And taken, in a lifetime's death in love,
> Ardour and selflessness and self-surrender. . . .
>
> > "The Dry Salvages"

The degree of reality of an object for a particular person, Eliot believed, varies in direct proportion with "the experiences which cluster around it: an object is real, we may say in proportion to its relations outside of its objectivity."[7] Eliot thus understands knowledge to be a relation between knower and known. And although he is speaking here in terms of the realm of concrete objects, we can apply his observations to the realm of concepts as well. Just as Eliot would never deny that the "unreal" object qua object exists, we would not deny the existence of the still point as concept. Likewise, we would say that its intensity, its reality, depends upon the experiences of its thinker in conjunction with it. But the experience of a concept or a definition must not be confused with the experience of a sunset, a sculpture, or a meeting with an old friend. The former exists primarily in the realm of the abstract, the latter in the realm of the concrete (which is, of course, mediated by mind).

The still point does refer to the Christian system of belief, and few would deny that,[8] but it does not belong exclusively to this system. Mallarmé, as Hugh Kenner has pointed out,[9] stands within the *Four*

Quartets just as Dante stands behind them, or above them. We see this in the celebrated still point passage in section II of "Burnt Norton," which I quote in the Introduction, and also in the following passage from section V:

> Words move, music moves
> Only in time; but that which is only living
> Can only die. Words, after speech, reach
> Into the silence. Only by the form, the pattern,
> Can words or music reach
> The stillness, as a Chinese jar still
> Moves perpetually in its stillness.
> Nor the stillness of the violin, while the note lasts,
> Not that only, but the co-existence,
> Or say that the end precedes the beginning
> And that the end and the beginning were always there
> Before the beginning and after the end.

At work here is the symbolist aesthetic, understood primarily not as a doctrine of correspondences but as a theory of linguistic construction whose elements refer to nothing but themselves and the system that they create. It is the pattern of the words that reaches into the stillness, not man.

Mallarmé, we remember, believed, as he said in his 1894 lecture "Music and Literature," that "Literature *does* exist and, I may add, exists alone and all-exclusively."[10] Mallarmé believed that all literature aspires toward the condition of music, which alone possesses purity of structure and form. We read in the *Four Quartets*—and Mallarmé would surely have agreed—that

> Words strain,
> Crack and sometimes break, under the burden
> Under the tension, slip, slide, perish,
> Decay with imprecision, will not stay in place,
> Will not stay still.
>
> "Burnt Norton"

Mallarmé's method was to still the voice of the poet and allow the words themselves, as he put it, to take the initiative. His method was to pass from the concrete to the pure "Idea," to conceive of an object in its absence, in its silence, to divorce it from "the direct and the palpable,"[11] to allude and suggest, to, as Charles Mauron has phrased it, evaporate reality into a musically fluid dream.[12] In his famous essay "Crisis in Poetry," Mallarmé describes the ineffable, the mystery, which is released by poetry:

> When I say: "a flower!" then from that forgetfulness to which my voice consigns all floral form, something different from the usual calyces arises, something all music, essence, and softness: the flower which is absent from all bouquets. . . .
> Out of a number of words, poetry fashions a single new word which is total in itself and foreign to the language—a kind of incantation. Thus the desired isolation of language is effected; and chance (which might have governed these elements, despite their artful and alternating renewal through meaning and sound) is thereby instantly and thoroughly abolished.[13]

In the still point passages from "Burnt Norton" we see a similar strategy at work. Although Eliot is not concerned to evoke an object, he is concerned to invoke a concept. He does so by beginning with abstraction, the name, "the still point." Then he evokes its quality through incantation and imagery, and finally he allows the concrete image to dissolve, leaving only the pattern and the Word. Eliot achieves what Mallarmé desired: "a single new word which is total in itself and foreign to the language—a kind of incantation." And in this sense the still point has no referent, it is the thing itself.

The still point thus reconciles opposites in two different ways—through the word itself, the system of language and art, and through the Christian religion, a system of articulated correspondences. The still point, in other words, has more than one vanishing point. It disappears into the poem, it disappears beyond the poem. Like an Escher engraving where the perspective of the picture plane is skewed and stairs lead in irreconcilable directions, the still point wavers between image and concept, taking on different meanings at different points in the poem. It is a supreme balancing act, an occupation only for great poets.[14]

If the still point, in either of these two cases, is not a symbol which is "lived into," what is possible in Eliot's world? In "The Dry Salvages" we read that

> For most of us, there is only the unattended
> Moment, the moment in and out of time,
> The distraction fit, lost in a shaft of sunlight,
> The wild thyme unseen, or the winter lightning
> Or the waterfall, or music heard so deeply
> That it is not heard at all, but you are the music
> While the music lasts.

Many of these moments "in and out of time" are recorded in the *Four Quartets*. Above all, we should not understand them as miniature versions or miniature visions of the still point. The two orders are similar but not the same. What separates them surgically is this: the still point is not to be experienced in the commonsense notion of the term (either it is to be strived for, but never reached, or it is to be suggested by, embodied in, art), while the unattended moments exist, or can exist, in an experiential dimension.

In his essay on Pascal, Eliot speaks of illumination, observing that "what can only be called mystical experience happens to many men who do not become mystics," noting that "you may call it communion with the Divine, or you may call it a temporary crystallization of the mind."[15] It is the latter formulation that most clearly conveys the status of unattended moments: they fall basically into the realm of cognition rather than that of divine communion. And here we are reminded of F. H. Bradley's epistemology, to which Eliot owed so much.

Bradley, we remember, denied that there is any actual dichotomy between the observer and the observed, desire and the desired. In his dissertation on Bradley, Eliot explains Bradley's notion of "immediate experience." "In feeling the subject and object are one,"[16] and

> immediate experience, we have seen, is a timeless unity which is not as such present either any*where* or to any*one*. It is only in the world of objects that we have time and space and selves. But the failure of any experience to be merely immediate, by its lack of harmony and cohesion, we find ourselves as conscious souls in a world of objects.[17]

Immediate experience is thus characterized by wholeness, by the union of the self with the other. But Eliot does not by any means discount the role that (self-) consciousness plays. In fact, he argues that consciousness is the necessary agent in the second step that we take in arriving at knowledge. As he explains, "We perceive an object, we will say [immediate experience], and then perceive it in a special relation to our body [the body defined as both physical and mental self, the conscious self being a construction]."[18] Bradley put it this way, and Eliot quotes him: "There is an immediate feeling, a knowing and being in one, with which knowledge begins."[19]

Knowledge *begins*. Immediate experience, or feeling, is wider than consciousness, for the conscious subject necessarily falls partly outside the whole of any feeling. As Eliot concludes: "We must therefore expect to find consciousness to be both something immediately given and something which would not be in the immediate experience unless it also extended beyond it. Consciousness is not an entity, but an aspect, and an inconsistent aspect of reality."[20] And since knowledge is a function of consciousness, it also lies both inside and outside of immediate experience. Moreover, since consciousness is an aspect of reality that Eliot believes does develop, we are free to assume that knowledge too can grow and develop. In referring to the development of consciousness, Eliot makes an interesting observation about the growth of the arts and the aesthetic self: "It is perhaps epistemology (although I offer this only as a suggestion, and to make clearer the sort of thing that I mean) that has given us the fine arts; for what was at first expression and behaviour may have developed under the complications of self-consciousness, as we become aware of ourselves as reacting aesthetically to the object."[21] All of this has special relevance to the unattended moment.

Wallace Stevens knew, as he wrote in the title poem of *The Rock*, that "It is an illusion that we were ever alive." Eliot too believes in the essential discontinuity of experience. On the one hand, he suggests that knowledge is cumulative; on the other hand, in "East Coker," he questions its value, since every appraisal of the past yields a different pattern:

> There is, it seems to us,
> At best, only a limited value
> In the knowledge derived from experience.

> The knowledge imposes a pattern, and falsifies,
> For the pattern is new in every moment
> And every moment is a new and shocking
> Valuation of all we have been.

For "consciousness and its object," as he puts it, "are both only evanescent aspects in reality."[22]

This evanescence of immediate experience, this essential discontinuity, is just what we encounter in the *Four Quartets*. As a group, the unattended moments are distinguished by a marvelous eclectic mysticism, or we could say, a mystical eclecticism. Together they pinpoint several peaks in Western literary history: the metaphysical poets, the Hesiodic tradition, naturalism, and English landscape romanticism.

In the rose-garden of "Burnt Norton," for example, Eliot gives us the imaginary recollected, not through emotion or tranquility, but through intellection. The way into the garden, into fantasy, is through ratiocination:

> Time present and time past
> Are both perhaps present in time future,
> And time future contained in time past.
> If all time is eternally present
> All time is unredeemable.
> What might have been is an abstraction
> Remaining a perpetual possibility
> Only in a world of speculation.
> What might have been and what has been
> Point to one end, which is always present.
> Footfalls echo in the memory
> Down the passage which we did not take
> Towards the door we never opened
> Into the rose-garden. My words echo
> Thus, in your mind.

We think of the English metaphysical poets, for Eliot's praise of their ability to associate thought and feeling is renowned. But here we find a peculiar version. Here thought does not so much blend with feeling, as logic yields to feeling, reverie, image, immediate experience. And in the rose-garden passage we see that for this imaginary, displaced ex-

perience to be complete, in order to invent history and the impossible
future, immediate experience must self-consciously be made conscious. It must be remembered:

> Time past and time future
> Allow but a little consciousness.
> To be conscious is not to be in time
> But only in time can the moment in the rose-garden,
> The moment in the arbour where the rain beat,
> The moment in the draughty church at smokefall
> Be remembered; involved with past and future.
> Only through time time is conquered.

Here "consciousness" must be understood as "immediate experience," as an intense sense of reality, as continuous, as out of time and
history, unanalyzable into parts.

But this experience dissolves:

> So we moved, and they, in a formal pattern,
> Along the empty alley, into the box circle,
> To look down into the drained pool.
> Dry the pool, dry concrete, brown edged,
> And the pool was filled with water out of sunlight,
> And the lotos rose, quietly, quietly,
> The surface glittered out of heart of light,
> And they were behind us, reflected in the pool.
> Then a cloud passed, and the pool was empty.

To preserve immediate experience, the self-conscious subject must
construct it as *an* experience, must react aesthetically to the experience
as one would to an object.

The method is presented abstractly, as we would expect from Eliot,
but the image is a thing of magic. In this passage we see Eliot's genius
more clearly, in fact, if we compare his capturing of imaginary experience with Williams' deliberate construction of an imaginary object, the
unicorn at the center of a virgin-and-whore scenario in the fifth book of
Paterson. Williams tries to trap the unicorn in the concrete of tapestry,
keeping the icon separate from him. By contrast Eliot's rose-garden is
psychological, unstable, flickering, like the flux of Wallace Stevens'
world.

In "Burnt Norton" we are presented with the reality of the imaginary which was never actual. In "East Coker" we encounter an historical vision of mythical cast. The sixteenth century surfaces in the twentieth, although how or why we cannot guess. The prerequisite for this privilege, however, and it is twice-repeated, is a peculiar one for Eliot: one must not disturb the past, one must not modify it, one must not come too close:

> In that open field
> If you do not come too close, if you do not come too close,
> On a Summer midnight, you can hear the music
> Of the weak pipe and the little drum
> And see them dancing around the bonfire
> The association of man and woman
> In daunsinge, signifying matrimonie—
> A dignified and commodious sacrament.

This moment is not so much a part of the historical record (and thus, given Eliot's understanding of how the present and past modify one another in endless reverberation, subject to change) as it is outside of history, existing as a utopian hesiodic moment, which can be eternally recovered by the literary imagination but cannot be entered. The time traveler is not free to join the dance. He can only observe. An invisible wall separates the literary anthropologist from this agricultural community. And this invisible wall, we might guess, is consciousness of the second degree.

But the Brueghel-like dance, a timeless round from the annals of primitivism, vanishes, to be replaced in "The Dry Salvages" by a new system of belief. Here we meet turn-of-the-century naturalism, the eternal gods of the sea and river calling up a timeless zone:

> The tolling bell
> Measures time not our time, rung by the unhurried
> Ground swell, a time
> Older than the time of chronometers, older
> Than time counted by anxious worried women
> Lying awake, calculating the future,
> Trying to unweave, unwind, unravel
> And piece together the past and the future,

Between midnight and dawn, when the past is all deception,
The future futureless, before the morning watch
When time stops and time is never ending;
And the ground swell, that is and was from the beginning,
Clangs
The bell.

And later in this Quartet, in the last section of "The Dry Salvages," Eliot casts a glance at nineteenth-century English landscape romanticism, at the unexpected moment of "immediate experience" sparked by "a shaft of sunlight / The wild thyme unseen, or the winter lightning."

All of these moments, from the rose-garden to the wild thyme, provide, are, "crystallizations of the mind," moments of cognition, of wholeness. And so too is the moment of religious pilgrimage in "Little Gidding":

Here, the intersection of the timeless moment
Is England and nowhere. Never and always.

Such moments populate the *Four Quartets*. They constitute a kind of catalogue of possible mystical experience. The *Four Quartets* do not form, in other words, a unified system that is suspended from a Christian or Buddhist point of view in the way that a Calder mobile hangs from a wire string. Rather, Eliot's genius is that he offers us so many different notions and nuances of language and holds them together suspended, as particles are, in solution.

But his medium is a particular one: it is literary. Eliot believes that the purpose of criticism is to establish a tradition, to forge continuity with the literary past, and it is in this way that the unattended moments function in the poem. They convince us that the poem is not solely a Christian poem with Eliot sloughing his way on to reconciliation of fire and roses as doggedly as Bunyan's famous pilgrim made his progress toward heaven. And they succeed as magic in great part *because* of their insubstantiality, their amazing incorporeity, their lack of hardy autobiographical roots. They exist—we do not deny that—but how, we need to ask, and for whom? For as Hegel said, there is nothing behind the curtain other than that which is in front of it.

The elusiveness of Eliot's voice is well known. Hugh Kenner has brilliantly discussed this aspect of Eliot's work in his aptly titled book *The Invisible Poet*. Kenner shows that in his earlier poems Eliot deals in verbal effects, not ideas, and as a result images and phrases are often unanalyzable, nonsensical.[23] In some of the earlier poems, including "Ash Wednesday," the reader tries to part the words from each other, only to find nothing there. The tissue of words closes in upon itself. The signifier displaces the signified. Words do not describe but curiously evoke, and often in the manner of, surprisingly enough (for her egotism is as obtrusive as Eliot's is not), Gertrude Stein. In the *Four Quartets* Kenner concludes, and I think rightly so, that we find poetry which is for the first time "selflessly transparent."[24] It is a final triumph of style where the Eliot of many masks disappears in favor of a disembodied voice of unquestionable authority.

We cannot help but contrast this voice, almost sphinxlike, with that of Pound's in the *Pisan Cantos*. Pound is alternately irascible and exhausted ("Oh let an old man rest"), irreverent ("Athene cd/ have done with more sex appeal"), irate as well as wise. Pound shows us himself.

On the other hand, as William Moynihan has put it, "the speaker of the poem is a fictive Eliot... old, dry, philosophic, religious, and most important, a poet."[25] Many have said that the *Quartets* are the most personal of Eliot's poems, yet the speaker is curiously absent. We find, with Kenner, that "the first person pronoun prompts no curiosity."[26] We find that these moments "in and out of time" exist apart from him. The "I," we feel, is not T. S. Eliot. The "I," in fact, is often not "I," but "we" and "you." One pronoun glides into another, effortlessly, and we follow, but we do not know whom we are following. Moreover we follow the voice into a dimension that is hypothetical, neither ideal or real.

Consider the "Little Gidding" sequence. The last poem of the *Four Quartets* opens in a spring that is not an actual spring but instead a vagary of winter (we think of Stevens' last poem in *The Rock*, where spring *is* spring). The first stanza closes with a call (a lament?) for the ideal:

> Where is the summer, the unimaginable
> Zero summer?

The time is out of joint. This is not peace but ''pentecostal fire / In the dark time of the year.'' Furthermore, the next two passages begin in the conditional:

> If you came this way,
> Taking the route you would be likely to take
> From the place you would be likely to come from,
> If you came this way in may time, you would find the hedges
> White again, in May, with voluptuary sweetness.

And,

> If you came this way,
> Taking any route, starting from anywhere,
> At any time or at any season,
> It would always be the same: you would have to put off
> Sense and notion.

And finally, throughout the entire first section of ''Little Gidding,'' the first person pronoun not only prompts no curiosity, it is literally missing.

As with the other timeless moments, Eliot is not here. He is absent, just as the thrush in the rose-garden, as David Ward has pointed out, is ''any thrush or no thrush; an ideal thrush, a thrush of memory or imagination; not even a thrush at all, but a way of expressing a movement of the soul.''[27] The particular has disappeared (did it ever exist?). The dialect of the tribe is purified.

And the *Four Quartets* as a whole possess this quality of the ephemeral. Although the names of each of the Quartets are place names, it is hard to associate each poem with a name (who can remember or rehearse what ''happens'' in each poem?). And it is even more difficult to remember what particular place is associated with what name. Again the signifier is detached from the signified and referent, lifted away by unknown hands from the concrete world. The words are talismans, not markers or signposts. The unattended moments do not have a locus in time and space, they do not have coordinates, nor are they meant to. This is part of their definition. For immediate experience is ''a timeless unity.''[28]

This is the magic of such moments: this also divests them of actuality. As readers, like the women in *Murder in the Cathedral*, we both know and do not know. We are both satisfied and unsatisfied. Just as the ''we'' of ''Burnt Norton'' must return to the rose-garden, we must return to the poem to find it again. The unattended moments exist as perpetual possibilities. Taken together they do not form a track which we feel Eliot himself followed. In Euclidean geometry two points make a line. In the *Four Quartets* these moments, hypothetical, do not make a Poundian periplum. And the Chapel Perilous lies either inside the poem, where Eliot is not, or outside the poem, where Eliot cannot reach.

II. CONSCIOUSNESS AND THE SOCIAL BOND

The World is trying the experiment of attempting to form a civilized but non-Christian mentality. The experiment will fail; but we must be very patient in awaiting its collapse; meanwhile redeeming the time; so that the Faith may be preserved alive through the dark ages before us; to renew and rebuild civilization, and save the world from suicide.— ''Thoughts after Lambeth,'' 1931[29]

Oh, I suppose the only thing to be done about W. civilization is to think as clearly as one can.—Letter to Bonamy Dobrée, November 12, 1927[30]

Unlike *The Rock* of Wallace Stevens, and within that book of poems the Roman convent that offers Santayana sanctuary, the world of the *Four Quartets* is not limited to the private meditative world of the individual. The nightmare world of urban industrialization and war intrude. We see London, its miles of subway tunnels and streets littered with garbage and buildings razed by bombs. This is as much a part of the *Four Quartets* as the hyacinth garden is of ''The Waste Land,'' perhaps more. The unattended moments, in fact, could be said to evaporate while the ''drifting wreckage'' remains constant:

> Men and bits of paper, whirled by the cold wind
> That blows before and after time,
> Wind in and out of unwholesome lungs
> Time before and time after.
>
> > ''Burnt Norton''

The question we must pose is: What is the relationship between the model for personal wholeness (whether or not it is either achievable or achieved) and the social vision of the poem? For we see that there is a disparity between what is possible for the individual and what is possible for an entire society.

The still point is rich in meaning for the individual in metaphysical and cognitive dimensions, but not in the social sphere. In the *Four Quartets* we find no corresponding model for a utopian society. The field of folk in "East Coker" is the only possibility, but if we compare it with Pound's Wagadu and Williams' Tenochtitlan, we can see that it does not at all function in the same way. Like the laughing children in the leaves of the apple-tree in the *Four Quartets*, the dancers are a literary vision, not an anthropological or historical text.

Whereas both Pound and Williams believed in the social systems of Africa and the Aztec as having literal relevance for their time, Eliot is primarily interested in the zestful dancers as a simple metaphor for social harmony. He was much more cautious, more judicious, prudent, and tentative than either of them. He possessed a much stronger reality principle than either of them. He wrote in terms of "Notes toward a Definition of" rather than an assertive "Guide to." If Pound's and Williams' strength is that they both believed in a direct link between poetry and social change, Eliot's strength is that he did not. Poetry for him could not legitimately deal with social ideals. As he wrote in *After Strange Gods,* "I should say that in one's prose reflexions one may be legitimately occupied with ideals, whereas in the writing of verse one can deal only with actuality."[31]

In prose, ideals perhaps, but not utopias. Eliot's temperament was ever purgatorial, not utopian. As he warned in *The Idea of a Christian Society,* the "prospect involves, at least, discipline, inconvenience and discomfort: but here as hereafter, the alternative to hell is purgatory."[32] From Eliot's extensive prose writing, especially the work that flanks and penetrates the time of composition of the *Four Quartets* (*After Strange Gods* was published in 1934, *The Idea of a Christian Society* in 1940, and *Notes toward a Definition of Culture* in 1948), we are familiar with his views as to why contemporary society was in such a desperate state of disintegration and what was necessary to hold society together.

For him, industrialism, the pursuit of private profit, and the all-pervading philosophy of materialism were the prime causes, and for him religion the strongest—in fact, the only—meaningful and effective social bond. In both of these areas of discussion Eliot is lucid, almost eloquent. He is less clear on the issue of what a better society would be, could be, like.[33] Unlike Pound or Williams he could not visualize it, he could not image it, in prose. All we are granted, essentially, are a few parameters: that on the local level he favored the small community with a strong tie to place and a stable hierarchical social structure bound together by Christianity, and that on the global level he accepted cultural pluralism, or as he aptly termed it, "an ecology of nations."[34]

Although Eliot wished to revive Christianity, and for this we would surely call him romantic, in his own terms it is not he, but people like Pound, who are the romantics. For Eliot separates things carefully, into categories; Pound does not. Eliot's 1919 review of Wyndham Lewis' novel *Tarr* is telling in this regard. What he says of the main character we can imagine him saying of Pound:

> His literature and his politics and his country life are one and the same thing. They are not in separate compartments, they are one career. Together they make up his real world: literature, politics, riding to hounds. In the real world these things have nothing to do with each other.[35]

A doctrine of segregation, poetics in one genre, politics in another.

Thus, the *Four Quartets* is lopsided, dislocated. Eliot could not build a poem on a model analogous to that of the Elizabethan world view where individual harmony is implicit in social harmony and both are implicit in cosmic harmony. Pound could, for he put one foot outside of his tradition and chose Confucius as a guide. Pound was at heart a *bricoleur*. But this Eliot could not be. To learn another tradition, to go to the center of it, "would require forgetting how to think and feel as an American or a European," Eliot fastidiously believed, and this was, of course, unthinkable.[36] Thus, the parts of the *Four Quartets* are discontinuous, each is not implicit in the other.[37] Harmony on the individual level cannot find its counterpart in society. "Hints and guesses" of a religious bond are all there are, and they are not enough to hold together the individual and society (or, to rephrase and thus reconstruct the problem in a better way, the organism and its organization).[38]

All that can be reasonably hoped for, in the world of the *Four Quartets,* is that the individual preserve the faith. And, almost ironically, this requires one to all but sever ties with others, to detach oneself. The artist, the man of religion, is thus, to use Victor Turner's phrase, a liminal man who exists outside of the ongoing social structure which, in Eliot's case, is industrial and technological society. But whereas for Pound this arena is communal *and* sexual *and* literary *and* natural, for Eliot the possibilities are much more limited.

If Eliot cannot offer us a vision of a utopian society in the *Four Quartets,* he does give us a model for individual growth and development. The ultimate goal is enhanced spirituality and peace. What *is* possible is increased consciousness. The method is three-fold: religious discipline ("the rest / Is prayer, observance, discipline, thought and action," we read in "The Dry Salvages"), the "hints and guesses" of the unattended moments, and research.

Research: this is what we would expect from a poet who is one of our greatest, and one of our most scrupulous, literary critics. This is in great part what Eliot means by exploration. The way back to the garden, to the beginning of the poem, to the source of creativity, which is desire and thus movement, is both hard work and its opposite, "inattention and detachment." In such a rose-garden moment, Eliot wrote in his essay on John Marston, is found the "kind of pattern which we perceive in our own lives only at rare moments of inattention and detachment, drowsing in sunlight."[39]

Here Eliot and the Stevens of *The Rock* agree on method, if not on the pattern or what is perceived. We must look and not look, hear and not hear:

> At the source of the longest river
> The voice of the hidden waterfall
> And the children in the apple-tree
> Not known, because not looked for
> But heard, half-heard, in the stillness
> Between two waves of the sea.

And thus at the end of "Little Gidding" we are returned to the rose-garden of "Burnt Norton," but it is a hypothetical return, a return predicted for the future:

> And all shall be well and
> All manner of thing shall be well
> When the tongues of flame are in-folded
> Into the crowned knot of fire
> And the fire and the rose are one.

It is a promise of peace, of reconciliation of beauty and suffering in the eternally projected future. One does not attain that, but one can possess consciousness. And the *Four Quartets* posit that growth.

The high value that Eliot placed on the development of consciousness as a measure of growth is seen not only in this poem but in many other places as well. Throughout his prose the terms ''conscious'' and ''unconscious'' appear and reappear like fetishes. A passage such as the following, from ''The Function of Criticism,'' is not unusual:

> A common inheritance and a common cause unite artists consciously or unconsciously: it must be admitted that the union is mostly unconscious. Between the true artists of any time there is, I believe, an unconscious community. And, as our instincts of tidiness imperatively command us not to leave to the haphazard of unconsciousness what we can attempt to do consciously, we are forced to conclude that what happens unconsciously we could bring about, and form into a purpose, if we made a conscious attempt.[40]

Just what meanings Eliot assigns to these terms throughout his work need to be untangled further, but here I can suggest a few of the areas which might be explored.

Biological evolution: Eliot has written, for example, that he accepts ''the development of consciousness in biological evolution as a development of knowledge.''[41]

The creative process: we are all aware of Eliot's description in ''Tradition and the Individual Talent'' of the poet's mind as catalyst, but we are perhaps less familiar with a variation on this theme that appears in Eliot's introduction to a 1929 collection of poems by Pound:

> The poet's progress is dual. There is the gradual accumulation of experience like a tantalus jar: it may be only once in five or ten years that experience accumulates to form a new whole and finds its appropriate expression. But if a poet were content to attempt nothing less than always his best, if he insisted on waiting for these unpredictable crystal-

lizations, he would not be ready for them when they came. The development of experience is largely unconscious, subterranean, so that we cannot gauge its progress except once in every five or ten years; but in the meantime the poet must be working; he must be experimenting and trying his technique so that it will be ready, like a well-oiled fire-engine, when the moment comes to strain it to its utmost.[42]

Just as in the *Four Quartets* the growth of consciousness requires discipline, research, and creative readiness for the unexpected moment, the creative process for Eliot makes the same demands. The "unpredictable crystallizations" of mind that are necessary for creation of form are indistinguishable from the unattended moments of the Quartets. The creative process and the intuitive cognitive process intertwine. The model for each is the same: the transformation of what is unconscious (but not necessarily the Freudian or Jungian unconscious) into consciousness. What is unformed is granted form. Consciousness is knowledge of form, and knowledge of form confers history:

> A people without history
> Is not redeemed from time, for history is a pattern
> Of timeless moments.
>
> "Little Gidding"

Significantly, however, the act of writing uncovers a message which the poet sends first to himself. In meditative poetry, Eliot says, the poet "does not know what he has to say until he has said it; and in the effort to say it he is not concerned with making people understand anything."[43] For Eliot, the unconscious, the subterranean, is thus identified as a source, a breeder, of knowledge. It is also associated with the vitality of the primitive in the area of language.

Language: the auditory imagination, we remember, is defined as "the feeling for syllable and rhythm, penetrating far below the conscious levels of thought and feeling, invigorating every word; sinking to the most primitive and forgotten, returning to the origin and bringing something back, seeking the beginning and the end."[44] The metaphor is that of the journey, and the very words recall the search in the *Four Quartets*: "In my beginning is my end." But poetry has a social function, and of this Eliot was always mindful.

The poet: according to Eliot, the poet is "more conscious" than "his people," other people.[45] The poet has a more refined sensibility and a clearer apprehension of feeling, and it is through our experience of form, the aesthetic experience, that he keeps alive our collective ability to feel.

Eliot, however, has a specific notion, a highly Eliotic notion, of the kind of knowledge that the word "consciousness" connotes. For him F. H. Bradley is one of the men who possesses such knowledge, which Eliot calls wisdom: "Of wisdom Bradley had a large share; wisdom consists largely of skepticism and uncynical disillusion; and of these Bradley had a large share. And skepticism and disillusion are a useful equipment for religious understanding and of that Bradley had a large share too."[46] The coolness and composure, the utilitarian and almost technological vocabulary ("useful equipment") that Eliot uses to describe the skeptical modern mind is striking, although not surprising. In the *Four Quartets* he speaks of "agony" but the tone is often professorial—abstract, parenthetical, and logical:

> Now, we come to discover that the moments of agony
> (Whether, or not, due to misunderstanding,
> Having hoped for the wrong things or dreaded the wrong things,
> Is not in question) are likewise permanent
> With such permanence as time has.
>
> "The Dry Salvages"

The wise mind, his own mind, cannot be free of skepticism and doubt. This is the burden of much of *The Elder Statesman* and Eliot's important essay on Pascal. In the latter we encounter slightly different terminology, but we must not let this mislead us, for Eliot makes essentially the same point. Skepticism of Montaigne's brand he condemns, and the radical doubt of Pascal he praises and would take as his model.

Pascal, he asserts, is the religious writer most relevant to us: "I can think of no Christian writer, not even Newman, more to be commended than Pascal to those who doubt, but who have the mind to conceive, and the sensibility to feel, the disorder, the futility, the meaninglessness, the mystery of life and suffering, and who can only

find peace through a satisfaction of the whole being.''[47] The acceptance of Christianity by the individual is not so much accomplished by
a Kierkegaardian leap of faith as by a conscious and conscientious,
disciplined act of the mind. Thinking the problem through properly,
Eliot explains, leads one into faith. Thus, the intelligent believer of
today, the conscious believer of today, he affirms, must successfully
join doubt and skepticism with faith (but, it is not Santayana's animal
faith). It is this marriage of opposites that is one of the most important
in the *Four Quartets*. And it is one that is *not* figured in the still point,
for the still point, we remember, does not admit of skepticism or
doubt. It lies beyond man's ken, although it exists as an ideal to guide
him.

The still point can not be reached, although man must pretend that it
could be. Likewise, Eliot recognized that global Christendom was
unfeasible, but believed that we must act as if it were. This raises the
question of his model for cultural development. Do we find that the
process of cultural growth and development is analogous to that of
individual development and the creative process? The answer is basically yes, although it is a yes that must be firmly qualified.[48]

Comparison of Eliot's views with the ''Prolegomena to the History
of Primitivism'' by Arthur O. Lovejoy and George Boas, first published in 1935,[49] suggests how complex Eliot's notion of historical
development is. The classifications offered by Lovejoy and Boas are
rigorously schematic and logical, dividing primitivism first into
chronological primitivism and cultural primitivism, then into finitist
and infinitist theories, theories of undulation, decline, and ascent, and
so on. The point to be made, however, is that Lovejoy and Boas use
the words ''savage'' and ''primitive'' interchangeably, largely dismiss
cultural primitivism as escapism, and at no time mention consciousness as a measure of cultural development. Eliot, as we see in *Notes
toward a Definition of Culture,* does not begin by accepting these
axioms and thus cannot draw such sharply defined conclusions about
primitivism. His tone, in fact, if we compare it with that of the
passionate cultural historian of the seventies, William Irwin
Thompson, who in great part shares Eliot's analysis of Western development, is neutral and calm.[50]

On the one hand Eliot recognizes that primitive communities are characterized by social cohesion, a shared culture, and lack of specialization. He understands that as civilization grows more complex, class consciousness appears, and religion, science, art, and politics split and coagulate into separate institutions, which must deliberately, consciously battle each other for power. He does not lament this loss of unity but does comprehend that it is a genuine loss: "the one thing that time is ever sure to bring about is the loss: gain or compensation is almost always conceivable but never certain."[51] But, on the other hand, increased consciousness and skepticism accompany increased complexity of civilization as compensation. And finally, although in his view cultural specialization is not necessarily equivalent to cultural disintegration, he does observe that in the West specialization has begun to degenerate into irreparable fragmentation.

Eliot, in other words, does not hold a rigid theory of either general progress from the primitive to the "civilized" or, conversely, general decline from organic community to fragmented polity. As he says, "We do not assume that there is, over a long period, progress even in art, or that 'primitive' art is, as art, necessarily inferior to the more sophisticated."[52] In this respect he was ahead of his time.

The problem, however, is this. For Eliot the relation between religion and culture in an ideal state is one in which "people are unconscious both of their culture and their religion."[53] As he writes in his essay on "Religion and Literature," "What I want is a literature which should be unconsciously, rather than deliberately and defiantly Christian."[54]

But later in that essay he involves us in a contradiction: "It is not enough to understand what we ought to be, unless we know what we are and we do not understand what we are, unless we know what we ought to be. The two forms of self-consciousness, knowing what we are and what we ought to be, must go together."[55] This more or less mirrors the distinction between tradition and orthodoxy that Eliot makes in *After Strange Gods*: tradition is basically unconscious and does not possess the means to criticize itself, while orthodoxy is basically conscious. Tradition can not be deliberately put on, like a raincoat to protect oneself from the elements. But orthodoxy can—and

Eliot adopted it in the form of Anglicanism. However, orthodoxy is not strong enough to hold a specialized society together. In other words, what is unconscious can be brought into consciousness, but the process cannot be reversed. And while the former may be repeated in each individual, the latter is impossible, I believe, for a civilization: once a fundamental tradition has hardened into orthodoxy, it is impossible for it to dissolve into its former state of invisible tradition.

And this brings us to the key point of this discussion. Whereas for the individual,

> . . . the end of all our exploring
> Will be to arrive where we started
> And know the place for the first time,

such an accomplishment is impossible for a civilization. Collective consciousness cannot give us back a tradition that has been lost. The split between organism and organization, the individual and his specialized technological society at large, cannot be healed by a return to Christianity. A civilization cannot go home again. In the *Four Quartets* Eliot, whatever his dreams, does not lie to us. In "The Waste Land" ancient wisdom couldn't lift the curse, nor can it here. As Eliot says in *Notes toward a Definition of Culture,* "Understanding involves an area more extensive than that of which one can be conscious; one cannot be outside and inside at the same time."[56] Yeats wrote in his last letter that "man can embody truth but he cannot know it." Eliot would have agreed, but he also would have accepted the reverse proposition that "man can know truth but cannot embody it."

III. THE QUEST FOR COMMUNITY

> And what the dead had no speech for, when living,
> They can tell you, being dead: the communication
> Of the dead is tongued with fire beyond the language of the living
> Here, the intersection of the timeless moment
> Is England and nowhere. Never and always.
>
> "Little Gidding"

If, as Eliot believed, the act of writing releases a message hitherto unknown to the poet himself, if the poet "cannot identify this embryo until it has been transformed into an arrangement of the right words in the right order,"[57] we must ask what this message is in the *Four Quartets*. And to answer this question it is appropriate to ask where it is that Eliot qua Eliot appears in the poem. This in turn involves us in a definition of the meditative poem.

For most critics of Eliot, the poetry of meditation is understood as the language of abstraction.[58] But Eliot himself has a different notion of what meditative poetry is. For him it is poetry that we generally label "lyric" poetry, poetry of the first person.[59] This accords, in part, with Louis Martz' helpful notion of the meditative poem as drama wherein the poet seeks himself in himself, or as we might put it, projects a part of himself, an image of himself, in order to know himself.[60] We have already seen that in the *Four Quartets* Eliot as a character playing himself is not distinctly or directly identified with the unattended moments beginning with the "Burnt Norton" rose-garden and stretching to the churchyard in "Little Gidding." These moments exist in a timeless and in great part a spaceless dimension without him.

But there is one passage in the *Four Quartets*, a passage which has been called "one of his finest pieces of writing,"[61] where Eliot does appear: the "Little Gidding" dramatization of his meeting with "a familiar compound ghost." This scene, extraordinary for Eliot, combines the immediacy of anecdote with the truth of dream. Old Possum, the Eliot who all his literary life has championed the art of the impersonal, here lays aside that dictum. We remember his famous words of years earlier in "Tradition and the Individual Talent": "the more perfect the artist, the more completely separate in him will be the man who suffers and the mind which creates."[62] What is so moving in the ghost sequence is that the mind which creates is no less perfect, but the man who suffers is closer to us and more human.

If, as Helen Gardner has pointed out, "The Hollow Men" is in part a work that presents the crisis we call middle age,[63] then the *Four Quartets* deals directly with the crisis of old age. The message which Eliot sends himself, and us, is a message from the dead. Eliot assumes a "double part." He is both himself and the other. We see Eliot as a character bringing what is unconscious, what is beyond and below, into consciousness, into the present:

> So I assumed a double part, and cried
> And heard another's voice cry: 'What! are *you* here?'
> Although we were not, I was still the same,
>   Knowing myself yet being someone other—
>   And he a face still forming; yet the words sufficed
> To compel the recognition they preceded.

Kenner has observed that the mechanism of the Eliot plot is "the entry of Lazarus, the man who has crossed a frontier and come back: Harry with his Furies invading Wishwood, Sweeney the uninvited guest at the ragtime jollification, the Magi returning to a kingdom in which they are no longer at home, where an alien people clutch their gods."[64] But here there is a significant variation: Lazarus is greeted by a man of his own kind, he is not alone. The past is greeted by the present. The dream is that the literary tradition is continuous, not discontinuous, that it exists for a moment in space rather than time. And it is a moment of grace for them both. The "familiar compound ghost," like Stevens' Santayana and Pound's Confucius, represents the cultural tradition that Eliot has both learned from and become a part of. This scene condenses the truth that, as Octavio Paz puts it, "the poem is not literary form but a meeting place between poetry and man."[65] The figure is a master, a teacher, a wise old man.

The message he delivers is one that neither Pound nor Stevens could have received and only Eliot could have conceived. It is first and foremost purgatorial, the vision of old age is a bleak and bitter one:

> 'Let me disclose the gifts reserved for age
>   To set a crown upon your lifetime's effort.
>   First, the cold friction of expiring sense
> Without enchantment, offering no promise
>   But bitter tastelessness of shadow fruit
>   As body and soul begin to fall asunder.
> Second, the conscious impotence of rage
>   At human folly, and the laceration
>   Of laughter at what ceases to amuse.
> And last, the rending pain of re-enactment
>   Of all that you have done, and been; the shame
>   Of motives late revealed, and the awareness

> Of things ill done and done to others' harm
> Which once you took for exercise of virtue.
> Then fools' approval stings, and honour stains.'

This could be Shakespeare's Jacques speaking. Until, unless,

> 'From wrong to wrong the exasperated spirit
> Proceeds, unless restored by that refining fire
> Where you must move in measure, like a dancer.'

Skepticism and faith, the two together, wisdom: this is one form of knowledge the ghost possesses and this is the knowledge Eliot presumably was in need of. But if the Eliot of skepticism and despair yields to the Eliot of skepticism and faith, this is no surprise to us. It is a formal solution to a poetic problem which Eliot had come to terms with in his life some time before. This I will come back to later.

This moment differs significantly from those preceding it in the *Four Quartets*. It opens to include the contemporary wasteland while others do not. It was the war, we remember, that prompted Eliot to write poetry again, to write "East Coker" and to continue with "The Dry Salvages" and "Little Gidding." Appropriately then, this scene takes place in London in the predawn hour after an air raid, and together the two men form "a dead patrol," a watch over the city. They are its guardians. It is a ritual action which they perform. And as we know, the one who participates in a ceremony is like an actor who plays a part: everything is and yet everything is not. It is a supreme achievement, for in all of the *Four Quartets* this is the single section where Eliot is able to unite the two worlds of cultural disintegration and individual illumination.

Not surprisingly, the context is an aesthetic one. Moreover, it is not a weightless union of abstractions ("In my end is my beginning") but a concrete, tangible reconciliation of opposites achieved within the frame of a dramatic situation. This scene has specific historical coordinates of space and time, and yet "this intersection" is "nowhere" and has "no before and after."

This is what the vision is. We must also realize what it is not. Eliot's poetry is not a poetry of ecstasy. This section in "Little Gidding" does not dramatize a vision of Incarnation or of mystical contact with God. Eliot knew what his limitations were in a secular society, and he knew what his possibilities were. And accordingly, he presents us with a poet, not a prophet, who delivers a vaguely Christian message. This is, of course, exactly the role Eliot set for himself. Eliot could not write a *Bhagavad-Gita*, where Krishna manifests himself. Eliot is not a New Dante and could not send himself a Beatrice. Nor is he Pound; he could not en-vision the eyes of a goddess in this London landscape. But in the *Four Quartets* Eliot does move far beyond the empty allegory of "Choruses from 'The Rock.'" Whereas in "Choruses," the Rock is handed wooden lines to speak before an undefined audience, in the *Four Quartets* we find a situation which is both dramatic and imaginative.

But the satisfaction we feel in this passage is not only a literary one. The message of the "familiar compound ghost" may have Christian overtones for those who would hear them, but the whole of this brief drama has an important sociological meaning. Contemporary urban society, as reflected in its subway faces,

> . . . the strained time-ridden faces
> Distracted from distraction by distraction
> Filled with fancies and empty of meaning
> Tumid apathy with no concentration
>
> "Burnt Norton"

is impacted, a dull mass. The individual, as we know Eliot believed, is in great part "empty of meaning" because the forces of industrialism and secularism have uprooted him from his traditional, personal associations—family, church, guild, village—in which he had clearly defined status, a coherent set of moral beliefs, and fellowship. And nothing has filled this vacuum. The subway rider is a displaced person among other displaced persons. As the Chorus asked in "Choruses from 'The Rock'":

> When the Stranger says: "What is the meaning of this city?
> Do you huddle close together because you love each other?"
> What will you answer? "We all dwell together
> To make money from each other"? or "This is a community"?

There is a basic human need for community, observes Robert Nisbet in *The Quest for Community,* and it is a need which is all the more pressing in our century. "The problem," Nisbet argues, "lies in the realm of the small, primary, personal relationships of society—the relationships that mediate directly between man and his larger world of economic, moral, political and religious values."[66] Our traditional small social groups, which had functional significance and also provided moral cohesion, have atrophied, he points out, and no new associations have taken their place. Our need for them is a fundamental one, he urges, and with this Eliot would agree. In "Choruses from 'The Rock' " the notion of community that Eliot offers is exclusively a Christian one. In *The Elder Statesman* he explores the remaking of community on the level of the nuclear family and friends. But in the *Four Quartets* he stresses the importance of another kind of association. As a poet, he recognizes and dramatizes his need to belong to a literary community that possesses a strong tradition and plays a vital role in the present. In the ghost passage we do not see Eliot detached "from self and from things and from persons," and we are glad of it:

> I said: 'The wonder that I feel is easy,
>   Yet ease is cause of wonder. Therefore speak:
> I may not comprehend, may not remember.'

He might have written: "The ease that I feel is cause of wonder."

The "familiar compound ghost" contains many poets particularly important to Eliot—Dante and Dante's Arnaut and Yeats and Pound and Shelley and Mallarmé and Milton. Together, and including Eliot, they form a guild in which master passes on craft and wisdom to apprentice. Given Eliot's belief in "the indestructible barriers between one human being and another," as Kenner has put it,[67] this is as close as he ever allowed himself in poetry to break down that barrier. Here we cannot help but contrast Eliot's pale abstraction of these poets with Pound's almost literal calling out of their names, one by one, in the *Pisan Cantos*. But the relationship of poets is not purely literary. It is also, for Eliot, psychological, moral, and religious. And finally, it is social: for their common concern was, and is, language and speech and urging "the mind to aftersight and foresight" ("Little Gidding"). As this passage makes clear, it is in great part concrete association (however hallucinatory) with the living tradition which gives strength and makes the ongoing fight possible. The ghost is itself the "embryo" that comes into life "near the ending of interminable night." Consciousness brings resolve:

> Old men ought to be explorers.
> Here and there does not matter
> We must be still and still moving
> Into another intensity
> For a further union, a deeper communion
> Through the dark cold and the empty desolation
>
> "East Coker"

> And next year's words await another voice.
>
> "Little Gidding"

In contemporary society, Nisbet argues, one of the roles of small social associations is to act as a check against the totalitarian tendency of a mass society. And for Eliot this is the role of the literary community.

Thirteen years after Eliot finished the *Four Quartets* he gave an address at Hamburg University on "Goethe as the Sage."[68] His tone in that essay is personal and almost affectionate, and his voice is wise. In the *Four Quartets* he had written: "The only wisdom we can hope to acquire / Is the wisdom of humility: humility is endless." The virtue of humility is a great part of the Hamburg lecture, and its words help us understand the wisdom of the *Four Quartets*. It is possible, Eliot argues, to distinguish between the philosophy of a poet and his wisdom. Whether or not we can accept the beliefs of Dante or Shakespeare or Goethe, we can accept, he maintains, their wisdom:

It is precisely for the sake of learning wisdom that we must take the trouble to frequent these men; it is because they are wise men that we should try, if we find one of them, uncongenial, to overcome our aversion or indifference. Of revealed religions, and of philosophical systems, we must believe that one is right and the others wrong. But wisdom is λόγος ξυνός, the same for all men everywhere. . . . That the wisdom and the poetry are inseparable, in poets of the highest rank, is something I have only come to perceive in becoming a little wiser myself.[69]

It is this inseparability of wisdom and poetry that we find in the *Four Quartets*.

The distinctive nature of the "wisdom" of Eliot's last major poem must be pursued just a bit further, however. Eliot provided his generation with a *model* of wholeness in "the still point" (for them the phrase expressed the ineffable, although for us it may have, unfortunately, become a cliché). Pound, Stevens, and Williams each define for themselves a still point which is invested with the specific gravity of a long life, the particularity of a certain poetic problem, and personal urgency. But for Eliot, as I have argued earlier in this chapter, the still point remains a linguistic construction. It is only in the ghost passage of "Little Gidding" that Eliot is able to unite the private world of mystical illumination with the social world of violence. And this is especially important for us because his *doppelgänger* speaks of the impending violence of old age, presenting him with a vision which is terrifying and offering veiled counsel which is indeed wise, but, I believe, not heeded.

Earlier I said that the *Four Quartets* deals directly with the crisis of old age. They do, but they do more than that, and this twist of time in Eliot's imagination is also distressing. It is crucial for us in the twentieth century to project ourselves imaginatively into our own future, our old age, for as individuals we tend to repress old age psychologically just as industrial culture has devalued the elderly as a nonproductive group and pushed them out of sight. But the surfacing of old age, in Eliot's sense, in middle age is a chilling prospect, and this is just what we encounter in the *Four Quartets*. Eliot imposes a dark vision of old age on his middle years. He is, we would say, old before his time, and here we mean old in the pejorative sense. For Eliot was only forty-seven when "Burnt Norton" appeared in his *Collected Poems* and only fifty-five when he published the entire set of poems together as the *Four Quartets*. Thus we might more accurately conclude that the *Four Quartets* deals with the crisis of middle age as viewed through the distorting lens of a repulsive old age.

The *Four Quartets* confirms that Eliot has a strong sense of the life cycle and the sequence of generations, but it is one that is bizarrely truncated: the stress is on *physical* decay, never growth. In "Burnt Norton," for example, he turns a lifetime of decrepitude to advantage:

> Yet the enchainment of past and future
> Woven in the weakness of the changing body,

> Protects mankind from heaven and damnation
> Which flesh cannot endure.

A few lines earlier in the poem the still point is described as the point "where past and future are gathered," but while the locus of these different points of time is lovely in abstraction (they are "gathered" together), it is purgatorial in the concrete, "the changing body" where they are enchained.

F. R. Leavis has called this attitude of Eliot's a sin against the principle of life.[70] And indeed it is a funereal way of understanding that "In my beginning is my end." These words open the second Quartet, which refers us to Eliot's ancestry by its title: Eliot's family came to America from the village of East Coker, located in Southeast Somersetshire. But the poetic point that Eliot makes is general, not specific to his own psychological and social history, not directed at the influences of his family's origins on his development. Instead he submerges all autobigraphy in the continually crumbling arc of time. We would agree, I think, that to a large extent his perspective is "wise": what a generation creates must necessarily die, and within a given life time one devotes oneself, appropriately, to different tasks at different times (this is perhaps less understood by the young than the old):

> Houses live and die: there is a time for building
> And a time for living and for generation
> And a time for the wind to break the loosened pane
> And to shake the wainscot where the field-mouse trots
> And to shake the tattered arras woven with a silent motto.

We cannot help but notice, however, that Eliot places the weight of time on destruction, decay, and death.

The time for building, living, and generation in Erikson's conception of the life span (generativity means caring for one's children, nurturing the next generation, turning one's attention to those younger than oneself) contracts to a line and one-half and receives no figurative attention, whereas the entire last three lines of the opening stanza of "East Coker" turn to decay which is rendered imagistically, not merely stated. These images are familiar and contribute to a perhaps comforting tone of domestic melancholy and rural elegy, but earlier in the section there appears an image of decay that is disturbing in its surreal mixture of organic matter—the earth which has always been and will always be a compost of "flesh, fur and faeces." Surely this is not wise but disquieting instead, an unhealthy vision of the dissolution of life while it is still intact and distinct, specifically recognizable in its various forms (the earth "is already flesh, fur and faeces, / Bone of man and beast, cornstalk and leaf"). For Eliot, this is the middle way, which will persist to the end, into old age: the two are part of a continuum of decay.

I have dwelt on this at some length because although Eliot certainly possesses an acute sense of history, his sense of time in terms of his own life is severely impoverished. In the *Four Quartets* a sense of the future is not palpable, only an indefinite stretch of the middle way, which is a kind of death in life. When Eliot writes, "In my beginning is my end," I fear that the end has absorbed everything. We learn in "The Dry Salvages" that his life is one of endless ends, a kind of Sartrean hell from which there is no exit:

> There is no end, but addition: the trailing
> Consequence of further days and hours,
> While emotion takes to itself the emotionless
> Years of living among the breakage
> Of what was believed in as the most reliable—
> And therefore the fittest for renunciation.

Although only middle-aged—and this is still a time of building—Eliot portrays himself as paralyzed, particularly in terms of poetry and the future. At the same time, he dismisses the tranquility of the wise old man for himself—and for others. "Autumnal serenity," we read in the second section of "East Coker," is in fact lethargy, dullness of mind, a reliance on old insights and useless knowledge.

Eliot is "wise" to recognize his limitations in poetry (the limitations of language). And I do not at all find his admissions of inadequacy to be duplicitous, an exaggerated humility masking pride, as others have.[71] When Eliot writes of his attempts and failures over a period of twenty long years to use words in a supremely accurate way adequate to his time, I believe him and admire the unflinching accuracy of his perception and the significance he attributes to work in language:

                              each venture
          Is a new beginning, a raid on the inarticulate
          With shabby equipment, always deteriorating
          In the general mess of imprecision of feeling,
          Undisciplined squads of emotion. And what there is to conquer
          By strength and submission, has already been discovered
          Once or twice, or several times, by men whom one cannot hope
          To emulate—but there is no competition. . . .

I am in awe of his courage, the fierce demands he makes upon himself,
but I wish for more, an energy of action. Given the vast span of
history, Eliot may be "wise" to devalue his own anguish, to present it
clinically, as he does in "The Dry Salvages," effacing his own torment and asserting that time is no healer; but does this "wisdom" not
have an inordinate cost?

   Although we commonly observe that things must be placed in
perspective in order to be seen with clarity, the olympian summit of
Eliot's point of view so diminishes his self that he disappears before his
time. As we will see later in Wallace Stevens' "To an Old Philosopher
in Rome," such a perspective is appropriate, fitting, for a man of
Santayana's age who has done his work. And so is the mode of his
being, which is the meditative mode: detachment.

   But is not Eliot's detachment from his own life premature and thus
unwise? We read in the third section of "Little Gidding" that
"detachment / From self and from things and from persons" is a
method for liberating oneself from an impossible future and an equally
impossible past. Detachment, like memory, appears to be a way of
tranquilizing the present, protecting oneself from it:

                        This is the use of memory:
              For liberation—not less of love but expanding
              Of love beyond desire, and so liberation
              From the future as well as the past.

Is not memory overvalued in his middle age? Eliot does not write of
memory as a pleasure. Rather, it serves a "use"; his attitude toward it
is pragmatic. Memory is a strategy for annulling desire, the impulse
toward things, and persons, and the enhancement of the self. Why this
fear of desire? Why this emphasis on a stillness, which, for a middle-

aged poet of great talent, does not so much resemble the balance of Stevens' Santayana, for example, as it does a stasis, perhaps stagnation? Clearly nothing seemed possible—either his life in poetry or his marriage. That anguish he believed could only be relieved and that tormented self vanish by submitting it to a higher meaning—"that refining fire" to which the ghost refers and which presumably will order one's life, providing a disciplined pattern in which "you *must* move in measure, like a dancer" (the italics are mine).

> See, now they vanish,
> The faces and places, with the self which, as it could, loved them,
> To become renewed, transfigured, in another pattern.

Although it is ungracious of us to ask more of Eliot than he was capable of giving, on the other hand, I think he did not follow his own best advice, the advice of the ghost he sent himself. As we have seen, the ghost's last words do counsel him to submit himself to the discipline of Christianity. And the final section of "Little Gidding" rehearses that theme. It is common to conclude therefore that the end of the *Four Quartets* represents the successful completion of a spiritual journey in which "the fire and the rose are one." But here I agree with F. R. Leavis who complains that the *Four Quartets* ends on a note of declaration rather than poetic persuasion.[72]

However this is not my major point. For the ghost had more to say. His speech is divided into three parts: the last three lines, which invoke the Christian tradition and come as an abrupt coda to both the first part, which is concerned with the relationship of the poet to his work, and the second part, which, as we have already seen, is concerned with the psychic and physical horrors of old age. It is the first section that is most relevant to us here. Speaking with authority, the ghost declares that " 'Last season's fruit is eaten.' " This is not an unfamiliar theme to us—Eliot has acknowledged this throughout the poem. But the ghost elaborates:

> 'For last year's words belong to last year's language
> And next year's words await another voice.
> But, as the passage now presents no hindrance
> To the spirit unappeased, and peregrine

Between two worlds become much like each other,
So I find words I never thought to speak. . . .'

Our attention is focused on the present, the potential for a living tradition. The ghost, like Eliot, is wretched, his "spirit unappeased," but he represents the possibility of presence, of utterance, of speech whose words do and will reach into the silence.

This is, for me, the wisdom which the ghost imparts. Not the Christian religion, for Eliot had embraced that years earlier, both in his poetry and his actions, but rather the possibility of poetry for Eliot himself. It is as if Eliot is prompting himself to speak, in poetry, to continue his work, despite its problematics, to act. "So I find words I never thought to speak," says the ghost, himself astonished that the words for this time, that place could be found.

D. W. Harding, commenting on "Little Gidding," declares that the last section of the *Quartets* "suggests a serene and revitalized return from meditation to one's part in active living."[73] Action for Eliot: would that not have meant a life in poetry? As we learned from his essay on "Tradition and the Individual Talent," which he had written years earlier, he believed in the power of the poetic community to affect its culture in a meaningful way. And in the ghost sequence of "Little Gidding," he is finally able to dramatize that power poetically. But he does not follow his own advice. After the *Four Quartets* he leaves his life in poetry, unable to find a voice in the present, and the plays that follow do not fulfill the measure of his talent.

1. T. S. Eliot, *Selected Essays* (New York: Harcourt, Brace & World, 1964), p. 433.

2. Theodore Roszak, *Where the Wasteland Ends: Politics and Transcendence in Post-Industrial Society* (Garden City, N.Y.: Doubleday, 1973), 128–29.

3. T. S. Eliot, *Knowledge and Experience in the Philosophy of F. H. Bradley* (London: Faber and Faber, 1964), p. 167.

4. Eliot makes an interesting distinction between an idea and a concept. A concept, he writes in *Knowledge and Experience* (p. 46), "is a thing-in-itself; it can be suggested rather than defined, through more and more general ideas, but is at no point to be identified with these ideas. . . . And we must not confuse the development of the language with the development in concepts; for it would, I think, be more apt to say

that the development of language is the history of our exploration of the world of concepts.''

5. T. S. Eliot, *Collected Poems: 1909–1935* (New York: Harcourt, Brace and Company, 1936).

6. "Dante," in *Selected Essays*, p. 219.

7. *Knowledge and Experience*, p. 158.

8. To mention but a few. Ethel Cornwall in *The Still Point: Theme and Variations in the Writings of T. S. Eliot, Coleridge, Yeats, Henry James, Virginia Woolf, and D. H. Lawrence* (New Brunswick, N.J.: Rutgers University Press, 1962), p. 60, concludes that Eliot's still point is "the intellectualized presentation of a Christian concept. Union with the still point," she says, "is equivalent to union with God." Or, D. E. Maxwell: " 'The still point' is God, and represents a summary and reconciliation of all the paradoxical attributes of the symbols (the axle-tree, wheel, river, etc.) which at once depend upon it and help to illustrate its nature—they could be described as a symbolic substratum" (*The Poetry of T. S. Eliot* [London: Routledge and Kegan Paul, 1952], p. 176). Or, Morris Weitz: "The still point, of course, is the symbol of the Logos, but it is also the symbol of the Christian God" ("T. S. Eliot: Time as a Mode of Salvation," in *T. S. Eliot, Four Quartets: A Casebook*, ed. Bernard Bergonzi [London: Macmillan, 1969], p. 147). What I object to is the reductionist tendency of such findings: on the whole the *Four Quartets* have suffered severely from the wealth of academic nations and the criticism of demystification. The general tack of critics is to say that the still point is a symbol of something else and that the rose garden, revolving wheel, and so on, are in turn symbols of the still point—a clear fill-in-the-blank hierarchy, as well built as a plaster-of-paris parfait, and as devoid of life, translucency, and richness. The *Four Quartets*, we must not forget, has a singular ability to contain conflicting images, but unfortunately many critics have treated Eliot as though he were more Descartes than Pascal. Eliot, we remember, found the *esprit de géometrie* to be "excessive" in Descartes, and the *pensées* of Pascal, although fragmentary in form and expression, to cohere magnificently in thought.

9. Hugh Kenner, *The Pound Era* (Berkeley: University of California Press, 1971), p. 136. We might consider pushing this distinction and conclude that the still point lies not only on the vertical axis of *metaphor* but also on the horizontal axis of *metonymy*. In his famous essay on aphasia, Roman Jakobson calls attention to the two basic ways in which the elements of language operate: the selection of a sign among similar items (this relation of similarity he calls "metaphor" and we may imagine it as a vertical axis). See his "Two Aspects of Language and Two Types of Aphasic Disturbances," in Roman Jakobson and M. Halle, *Fundamentals of Language* (The Hague: Mouton, 1956), pp. 55–82. The most important works of Mallarmé—*Un Coup de Des* and *Le Livre*—do not fit the commonly accepted definition of symbolism as metaphoric substitution. Mallarmé's early work, in other words, employs a priori codes (as Eliot employs the code of Christianity), but in his later work Mallarmé images man as creator of new codes. Syntax, the creation of meaning by contiguity and context, assumes, in other words, a greater importance than the use of metaphor.

10. Stéphane Mallarmé, *Selected Prose Poems, Essays, and Letters*, trans. Bradford Cook (Baltimore: Johns Hopkins University Press, 1956), p. 47.

11. *Selected Prose Poems*, p. 42.

12. Stéphane Mallarmé, *Poems*, trans. Roger Fry (New York: Oxford University Press, 1937).

13. *Selected Prose Poems*, pp. 42–43.

14. In the strange opening passage of section II of "Burnt Norton," Eliot brings the two poles together—the vertical pole of metaphor and the horizontal pole of metonomy:

> Garlic and sapphires in the mud
> Clot the bedded axle-tree.
> The trilling wire in the blood
> Sings below inveterate scars
> And reconciles forgotten wars.
> The dance along the artery
> The circulation of the lymph
> Are figured in the drift of stars
> Ascend to summer in the tree
> We move above the moving tree
> In light upon the figured leaf
> And hear upon the sodden floor
> Below, the boarhound and the boar
> Pursue their pattern as before
> But reconciled among the stars.

Here Mallarméan syntactics and the contradictory medieval notion of correspondences are juxtaposed, and they cohere.

15. "The *Pensées* of Pascal," in *Selected Essays,* p. 358.

16. *Knowledge and Experience*, p. 21.

17. *Knowledge and Experience*, p. 31.

18. *Knowledge and Experience*, p. 155.

19. *Knowledge and Experience*, p. 28 (quoted from Bradley's *Essays on Truth and Reality* [Oxford: Clarendon Press, 1946], p. 159).

20. *Knowledge and Experience*, p. 28.

21. *Knowledge and Experience*, p. 155.

22. *Knowledge and Experience*, p. 156.

23. Hugh Kenner, *The Invisible Poet: T. S. Eliot* (New York: Harcourt, Brace & World, 1959). Kenner discusses this question, however, mainly from the point of view of the relation between the words and the "zone of consciousness" from which they emanate, not from the point of view of the relationship between the words and what they point to as signifier or referent. I would further observe, in fact, that often Eliot's poems are susceptible to the criticism he offers of Swinburne: "It is, in fact, the word that gives him the thrill, not the object. When you take to pieces any verse of Swinburne, you find always that the object was not there—only the word" ("Swinburne as Poet," in *Selected Essays,* p. 284).

24. *The Invisible Poet,* p. 293.

25. William T. Moynihan, "Character and Action in *Four Quartets,*" in *T. S. Eliot: A Collection of Criticism,* ed. Linda W. Wagner (New York: McGraw Hill, 1974), p. 75.

26. *The Invisible Poet,* p. 294.

27. David Ward, *T. S. Eliot, between Two Worlds: A Reading of T. S. Eliot's Poetry and Plays* (London: Routledge and Kegan Paul, 1973), p. 227.

28. *Knowledge and Experience,* p. 31.

29. *Selected Essays,* p. 342.

30. Quoted in Bonamy Dobrée, "T. S. Eliot: A Personal Reminiscence," in *T. S. Eliot: The Man and His Work,* ed. Allen Tate (New York: Dell, 1966), p. 75.

31. T. S. Eliot, *After Strange Gods* (London: Faber and Faber, 1934), p. 28.

32. T. S. Eliot, *The Idea of a Christian Society* (New York: Harcourt, Brace, 1940), p. 22.

33. See Stephen Spender's essay "Remembering Eliot," in *T. S. Eliot: The Man and His Work*: "Possibly, then, the centre of Eliot's work is its exploration of the truth that there cannot in our time be a synthesis between the modern city of the industrial world—bound entirely to the temporal and gambling every moment with destruction—and the eternal city with aims of civilization outside the temporal" (p. 63).

34. "We have not given enought attention to the ecology of cultures," he wrote in *Notes toward a Definition of Culture* (London: Faber and Faber, 1948), p. 58. This, we realize, some thirty years later, was a prescient, not a reactionary, statement to make.

35. Published in 1919 and quoted in *The Invisible Poet,* p. 113.

36. *After Strange Gods,* p. 41.

37. Compare with the last paragraph of "The *Pensées* of Pascal," *Selected Essays,* p. 368, from which the following is excerpted: "We cannot quite understand any of the parts, fragmentary as they are, without some understanding of the whole [Eliot is here referring to the form of Pascal's work]. Capital, for instance, is his analysis of the *three orders*: the order of nature, the order of mind, and the order of charity. These three are *discontinous*; the higher is not implicit in the lower as in an evolutionary doctrine it would be. In this distinction Pascal offers much about what the modern world would do well to think."

38. As used by Raymond Williams, this is much better terminology because it reveals the artificiality of treating these two terms as distinct from each other rather than as different aspects of a single system, which they are. See his *The Long Revolution* (New York: Columbia University Press, 1961), p. 100. See also his *Culture and Society, 1780–1950* (New York: Columbia University Press, 1958), which contains an excellent discussion and evaluation of Eliot's views of culture.

39. "John Marston," *Elizabethan Essays* (New York: Haskell House, 1964), p. 194.

40. *Selected Essays,* p. 13. What Neumann has to say about this in *Art and the*

Creative Unconscious, p. 159, is instructive: "The separation between the psychic systems, which becomes intensifed in the course of development, leads more and more to a defensive attitude of consciousness over against the unconscious, and to the formation of a cultural canon that is oriented more toward stability of consciousness than toward the transformative phenomena of possession. Ritual, which may be regarded as a central area of psychic transformation, loses its regenerative significance."

41. *Knowledge and Experience*, p. 17.

42. Ezra Pound, *Selected Poems* (London: Faber and Guner, 1928), p. 16.

43. T. S. Eliot, "The Three Voices of Poetry," in *On Poetry and Poets* (New York: Noonday Press, 1961), p. 107.

44. T. S. Eliot, *The Use of Poetry and the Use of Criticism: Studies in the Relation of Criticism to Poetry in England* (London: Faber and Faber, 1933), pp. 118–19. See also "The Music of Poetry," in *On Poetry and Poets*, pp. 31–32: the poet "has the privilege of contributing to the development and maintaining the quality, the capacity of the language to express a wide range, and subtle gradation, of feeling and emotion; his task is both to respond to change and make it conscious, and to battle against degradation below standards which he has learnt from this past."

45. "The Social Function of Poetry," in *On Poetry and Poets,* p. 9.

46. T. S. Eliot, "Francis Herbert Bradley," in *For Lancelot Andrewes* (Garden City, N.Y.: Doubleday, Doran, 1929), p. 79.

47. "The *Pensées* of Pascal," in *Selected Essays,* p. 368.

48. I disagree, therefore, with William Chace, who, in *The Political Identities of Ezra Pound and T. S. Eliot* (Stanford, Calif.: Stanford University Press, 1973), p. 200, argues that Eliot viewed consciousness as a central and impossible obstacle to the development of culture, and that Eliot is devoted to "consciousness negated, to the unconscious absorption of society by self, self by society," and that "all does gradually become One, just as in *Four Quartets.*"

49. Arthur O. Lovejoy and George Boas, "Prolegomena to the History of Primitivism," in *Primitivism and Related Ideas in Antiquity* (New York: Octagon Books, 1965), pp. 1–22.

50. Thompson offers a Jungian-Yeatsian theory, arguing that we have fallen from unity to multiplicity, that surplus and specialization have increased the distance between men in different roles, and that we are approaching a new phase in Western cultural development, which he calls the scientific-planetary civilization. This is, of course, where the prudent Eliot, not having a taste for futurology or speculation, could not follow. See "Values and Conflict Through History: The View from a Canadian Retreat," *At the Edge of History: Speculations on the Transformation of Culture* (New York: Harper and Row, 1971), pp. 104–50. Thompson, by the way, graces his dedication page with a quotation from the last stanza of "Little Gidding," and he records in his next book, *Passages about Earth: An Exploration of the New Planetary Culture* (New York: Harper and Row, 1973), a pilgrimage he makes to Lindisfarne, which echoes, as he was no doubt aware, the pilgrimage to Little Gidding.

51. *Notes toward a Definition of Culture,* p. 25.

52. *Notes toward a Definition of Culture,* p. 29. See also Eliot's essay "The

Modern Mind,'' in *The Use of Poetry and the Use of Criticism,* p. 122, in which he discusses the development of self-consciousness in poetry and the criticism of poetry beginning with Dryden and continuing into the twentieth century: ''I have not wished to exhibit this 'progress in self-consciousness' as being necessarily *progress* with an association of higher value. For one thing, it cannot be wholly abstracted from the general changes in the human mind in history; and that these changes have any technological significance is not one of my assumptions.''

53. *Notes toward a Definition of Culture,* p. 31.

54. *Selected Essays,* p. 346.

55. *Notes toward a Definition of Culture,* p. 353.

56. *Notes toward a Definition of Culture,* p. 41. Neumann puts it more strongly in *Art and the Creative Unconscious,* p. 167: ''Differentiation and hyperdifferentiation of consciousness down to the most dangerous one-sidedness and disequilibrium are the hallmarks of our culture, whose faulty balance can no longer be repaired solely by the natural compensation of the psyche. But a return to the old symbols, an attempt to cling to what still remains of the symbolic religious values, also seems doomed to failure. For our understanding of this symbolism, even our affirmation of it, implies that the symbol itself has departed from the numinous realm of the creative and entered into the sphere of conscious assimilation.''

57. ''The Three Voices of Poetry,'' in *On Poetry and Poets,* p. 106.

58. F. O. Matthiessen, for example, in *The Achievement of T. S. Eliot,* 3rd ed. (London: Oxford University Press, 1958), p. 183, identifies the opening of ''Burnt Norton'' as ''a meditation on time,'' and Helen Gardner, in *The Art of T. S. Eliot* (New York: E. P. Dutton, 1959), p. 38, equates meditation with abstract speculation. Less common is the view of A. Alvarez (''A Meditative Poet,'' in *T. S. Eliot, Four Quartets: A Casebook,* ed. Bernard Bergonzi, p. 240), with whom I am in complete agreement: ''He is, in some ways, a meditative poet. But this does not mean a poet who deals in abstractions; Eliot's meditations are meditations on experience, in which the abstractions belong as much as the images; they are all part of his particular cast of mind, the meaning he gives to past experience. But Eliot is, I think, a relatively indifferent, or uninterested, observer of the phenomenal world—though in his earlier poems he was a sharp observer of manners. He is instead a supreme interpreter of meditative experience.''

59. ''The Three Voices of Poetry,'' in *On Poetry and Poets,* p. 106.

60. *The Poem of the Mind,* p. 31.

61. Alvarez, ''A Meditative Poet,'' p. 240.

62. *Selected Essays,* pp. 7–8.

63. *The Art of T. S. Eliot,* p. 111.

64. *The Invisible Poet,* p. 31.

65. *The Bow and the Lyre,* p. 5.

66. Robert Nisbet, *The Quest for Community* (New York: Oxford University Press, 1953), p. 49. Eliot was not only aware of but approved of Nisbet's work, which he considered to be ''conservative'' (see ''The Literature of Politics,'' *To Criticize the*

Critic, p. 141). The title of the second section of this chapter is taken, in part, from the title of one of Nisbet's books (*The Social Bond: An Introduction to the Study of Society* [New York: Alfred A. Knopf, 1970]).

67. *The Invisible Poet,* p. 90.

68. *On Poetry and Poets,* pp. 240–64.

69. *On Poetry and Poets,* pp. 263–64.

70. See F. R. Leavis' commentary on "Little Gidding" in *The Living Principle: "English" as a Discipline of Thought* (London: Chatto and Windus, 1975). Leavis also singles out the ghost sequence as extraordinary to the *Four Quartets.* He observes that Eliot's experience as an air-raid warden during the Second World War "was a rude and salutary exposure to life—a kind of exposure necessary to a life-fearing potential major poet. In the Dantesque narrative Eliot *is,* and very impressively, a major poet; the complexity inseparable from its being so unmistakably creative evocation—organic, and in a way remote from assertion, so urgent—is not confined to the sensory vividness of the warden-poet's report.

"Nowhere else does Eliot come so close to full recognition of the realities of what he is—to full recognition that is, of the human nature that he shares, life being *in* himself" (p. 256).

71. See, for example, John Barker Muth, "The Patterned Pursuit: T. S. Eliot's *Four Quartets* and the Meditative Tradition" (Ph.D. diss., Rutgers University, 1976). I have only a few minor disagreements with Muth, whose scholarship on the *Four Quartets* I found very useful and his notion of wisdom as unlearning, provocative (we might wish to relate it to the principle of de-creation in Wallace Stevens).

72. *The Living Principle,* p. 256.

73. D. W. Harding, "Little Gidding," in *T. S. Eliot: A Collection of Critical Essays,* ed. Hugh Kenner (Englewood Cliffs, N.J.: Prentice-Hall, 1962), p. 128.

3

EZRA POUND AND THE *PISAN CANTOS*
The Teachings of Confucius
The Teachings of Ezra Pound

Sincerity, this precision of terms is heaven's process.
What comes from the process in human ethics. The sincere man finds
the axis without forcing himself to do so. He arrives at it without
thinking and goes along naturally in the midst of the process [T s'ung
yung chung tao], *he is a wise man. He who is sincere seizes goodness,*
gripping it firmly from all sides. —The Unwobbling Pivot[1]

The sincere man and the wise man, Pound learned from Confucius, finds his personal point of balance (his "still point," the "axis," the "unwobbling pivot") by means other than Western logic, reason, and the incessant abstraction of the mind. In the U.S.A. Detention Training Center north of Pisa in 1945, Pound discovered that "Le Paradis n'est pas artificiel." It is not unusual that this lesson and this discovery should come together, for they were, in fact, the two sides of the same coin, the two faces of the same open page. Pound, sixty years old and locked up in a hellhole of a wire cage, had only notebooks to keep him alive, and in these notebooks he worked on both translations of Confucius (*The Great Digest* and *The Unwobbling Pivot*) and the *Pisan Cantos* (the record of the making of a wise old man). The two literally interpenetrate and work together. But Confucius, although dominant, is not the only figure behind the *Pisan Cantos*. Pound commentators have been eager to appoint various heroines, Venus, for example,[2] or Persephone.[3] This hero(ine) hunting can only be misleading, for the important point is that in the *Pisan Cantos* there is, on the contrary, no *one* personage (either historical or mythical) and/or no *one* particular path which Pound takes to "le paradis."

Pound was in severe need of grace under pressure, and he looked for it and found it in as many places and in as many dimensions as possible: the natural landscape, personal memory, the third world, traditions of all kinds, the utopian imagination, the prisoners around him. In this way he is so unlike Williams, who in *Paterson V* proposed essentially only one way to counter old age and death: that of the museum, the modern tomb of dead civilizations.

Williams, in his reliance on slice-of-life imagism, on pictorial imagism, on "re-painting" the flowers in the Cloisters Tapestries, on a kind of sweet domesticity, failed. He failed in great part because the "art" he chose was unrelated and set apart from the culture in which he lived (the lower-class industrial city of Paterson), and he could not, as Pound could with his own choices of art of the past, make it new; he could not successfully reintegrate the traditions of the past into the culture of the present. In the end the Cloisters Tapestries of Williams remain merely beautiful, not immediately meaningful or useful. Pound, we remember, believed that "the setting of the museum above the temple is a perversion,"[4] and Pound is right. Williams lacked, at that crucial time in his life and his poetry, a sense of the divine, the religious, the sacramental. This is one of the reasons why his creaky symbolism of whore-virgin-and-unicorn did not work any better than his reweaving of the Tapestries. Williams, one concludes, tried to set the stage for experiencing in *Paterson V* what we could (not so generously) call a moment of *reassurance,* a moment possessing none of the religious qualities of Pound's conception of the "magic moment." But Williams only succeeded in talking around it, and perhaps in talking himself, but not us, into it.

Why could Pound achieve in the *Pisan Cantos* what Williams could not in *Paterson V?* In great part Pound's achievement was possible because of the "method" of the Cantos, their extreme openness of form. This is not as simplistic or as obvious as it might sound. Paradise, Pound says, is "spezzato," broken:

> it exists only in fragments unexpected excellent sausage,
> > the smell of mint, for example,
> > Ladro the night cat.

By this he means that an eternal, continuous paradise is impossible, never again possible (was it really ever possible?). He also means that it can exist, does still exist, in "unexpected" moments, fragments which not only point to something else, something larger, something beyond, but also *are* the " 'divine or permanent world.' "[5] What is important here is the concept of the unexpected. Pound's notion parallels that of Zen where a simple, unanticipated event (the falling of a petal, for example) can trigger, can invite *atasal*. One must be ready but one cannot be consciously looking. As Pound translated Confucius, the sincere man "arrives at it without thinking and goes along naturally in the midst of the process."[6]

This leads us to the chief difference between the openness of Pound's *Pisan Cantos* and that of Williams' *Paterson*. Although both are squarely in the American tradition of the open poem and although both find heirs in the Black Mountain poets and the Beats, Pound, however, had early on made a commitment about (and to) his poetry, a commitment crucial to the development of American poetry, which Williams never had. For Pound, the question of openness was not just a matter of the way the poem was allowed to look on the page. Nor was it only an acceptance of what had before been regarded as undesirable foreign matter—the mixing of prose and poetry, for example, or the injection of scraps from historical accounts into a lyric base. More importantly, for Pound the openness of the Cantos meant that the act of writing and his life were somehow one and the same. The two could not be neatly separated the way one could divide (and conquer) the Life and Works of T. S. Eliot or the Work and Writing of Wallace Stevens. The teachings of Confucius and the draft of the *Pisan Cantos* literally run through each other in the manuscript notebooks, and so do Pound's writing and his life. And just as life has no plot, neither do his *Pisan Cantos*. They are, even more so than the preceding Cantos, a kind of daybook, a journal, a form which, interestingly enough, became popular in American poetry in the sixties and seventies (think of Gary Snyder, of Paul Blackburn, of Allen Ginsberg).

To say this is not to say that Pound did not have a vague, general notion of the direction he wished the Cantos to take. He certainly did, and critics are fond of quoting from his famous 1927 letter to his father in the hallowed name of an articulate structure:

Have I ever given you outline of main scheme : : : or whatever it is?
1. Rather like, or unlike subject and response and counter subject in fugue.

 A. A. Live man goes down into world of Dead
   C. B. The "repeat in history"
   B. C. The "magic moment" or moment of metamorphosis, bust thru
          from quotidien into "divine or permanent world." Gods, etc.[7]

The model is the *Divine Comedy,* we could say, or the model is the *Odyssey.* A model is not the same as a plot, however. A model permits flexibility, it is an undercurrent, a substructure, a scaffolding on which the substance is built. A plot, on the other hand, is by definition the focus of attention in the genres which it dominates—the novel, the drama—but not in poetry. A plot is a chain of events (a *chain*), it is planned in advance. But Pound's Cantos are not a novel or a five-act drama with a neat dénouement. They are an unfolding of his life (Pound was among the first to invent this form; to my knowledge it is only Zukofsky in "*A*" who preceded him). Pound may have begun with the figure of Odysseus in the back of his mind, but he could not have anticipated the Second World War and the D.T.C. And that the model is latent, and best left so, is easily seen when we compare Pound's use of the homeomorph (to use Kenner's term)[8] with Williams' cumbersome and overweening use of metaphor in *Paterson*. Williams grafts the Giant onto the city of Paterson or the city onto the Giant, it little matters which. In the Cantos the journey of Odysseus resonates with the journey of Pound; the paradigm of the *Divine Comedy* works on a subliminal level (or would, if only commentators would not be so heavy-handed in digging it up).

Pound had, in fact, once said that the *Divine Comedy* was not an epic but rather a lyric, "the tremendous lyric of the subjective Dante,"[9] and the same is true of his own Cantos. In the *Pisan Cantos* especially, the act of writing upheld his life in a more immediate way than Mallarmé would ever have understood: "As a lone ant from a broken ant-hill / from the wreckage of Europe, ego scriptor" [LXXVI]. Writing for Pound was more than ever before a way of talking to himself ("to write dialog because there is/no one to converse with" [LXXX]) and of saving himself. The *Pisan Cantos* are nothing less than a survival piece.

Pound had long held the theory that you see nothing and find nothing if you start with a map, if you proceed into unknown territory with a plan in hand as to what is important, if you use someone else's guide, someone else's categories and abstractions. Territory, he believed, must remain unknown until personally explored so that the unexpected is possible. If the unexpected is possible, then the future (change and growth) is also possible. "Periplum," the method of charting life by points of experience, is a watchword of all of the Cantos, not just the *Pisan Cantos*.

But in the *Pisan Cantos* the word as mantra and the concept behind the word take on a more poignant meaning. Pound's dream for Italy had twisted into nightmare. He opens the sequence:

> The enormous tragedy of the dream in the
> peasant's bent shoulders
> Manes! Manes was tanned and stuffed,
> Thus Ben and la Clara *a Milano*
> That maggots shd/ eat the dead bullock
> DIGENES, διγενές, but the twice crucified
>   where in history will you find it?
>
> [LXXIV]

His Italy was gone. Pound himself had been stripped of his freedom, and his wife, and his books—all this by a country that he loved. He questioned his very future:

> we will see those old roads again, question,
>   possibly
> but nothing appears much less likely
>
> [LXXIV]

He had to start again, to find what he could live on. This is periplum with a vengeance. But in a way, this hell is just what made those fragments of Paradise possible.

"Periplum": in the *Pisan Cantos* it connects with Pound's notion of mysticism as being based on "direct perception":

> The flavours of the peach and the apricot are not lost from generation to generation, neither are they transmitted by book-learning. The mystic tradition, any mystic tradition, is of a similar nature, that is, it is dependent on direct perception, a 'knowledge' as permanent as the faculty for receiving it.[10]

As he wrote in *Gaudier-Brzeska: A Memoir,* "An image . . . is real because we know it directly."[11] Direct perception: what Pound accepted as a matter of course, Wallace Stevens debated his entire life. Was direct perception possible? Stevens fussed. At times he would answer no, arguing (reasonably, rationally, in the Lockean tradition) that the categories of the mind intervened (these categories could be logical, as in "Metaphors of a Magnifico," or metaphorical, as in "Someone Puts a Pineapple Together"). At times he would answer yes, yet add that plain-and-simple perception (the "painting" of carnations in "The Poems of Our Climate"), the fruit of imagism, was not enough.

In this Stevens and Pound agree. Pound had long ago articulated the canon of this brand of imagism, a "technical hygiene" as Hugh Kenner has so aptly labeled it:[12]

> 1. Direct treatment of the 'thing' whether subjective or objective.
> 2. To use absolutely no word that does not contribute to the presentation.
> 3. As regarding rhythm: to compose in the sequence of the musical phrase, not in sequence of a metronome.[13]

Like Stevens, Pound rejected this doctrine as being insufficient (Williams, however, never really did). But whereas Pound was always sure of alternatives, steady in his beliefs in the "Symposium of the Whole," to use Robert Duncan's words, Stevens was not. Pound was interested in the emotional as well as the intellectual component; we recall his "second" definition of the image: "An 'Image' is that which presents an intellectual and emotional complex in an instant of time."[14]

But Stevens was uneasy with the emotional, the personal, as a means of validating the "real." In one of his later poems, "Bouquet of Roses in Sunlight," for example, perception of the real (the object) is based on feelings, and this basis Stevens hastens to undermine:

> Say that it is a crude effect, black reds,
> Pink yellows, orange whites, too much as they are
> To be anything else in the sunlight of the room,
>
> Too much as they are to be changed by metaphor,

Too actual, things that in being real
Make any imaginings of them a lesser thing.

And yet this effect is a consequence of the way
We feel and, therefore, is not real, except
In our sense of it, our sense of the fertilest red,

Of yellow as first color and of white,
In which the sense lies still, as a man lies,
Enormous, in a completing of his truth.

What "we feel . . . is not real"; such experience only reflects ourselves (we think of Mallarmé gazing out of the window and seeing only his own image reflected); the room is one of solipsism. In his last poems Stevens is finally able to put aside the internal dialogue of the mind and accept without serious qualification "direct perception." The title of the last poem in the *Collected Poems* testifies to this: "Not Ideas about the Thing but the Thing Itself" (but it also testifies to his never having rejected Western dualism).

But the question to ask is: How does Stevens' concept of "direct perception" differ from that of Pound? For the difference is vast. Stevens' aesthetic is, finally, an aesthetic of glimpses,[15] of moments which give nourishment and an impulse to continue living. But for Stevens one moment does not connect with another, nor does the experience of a particular moment connect with something larger. For him the moment of perception is literally a fragment unto itself, not as for Pound a fragment which is a part of a whole. For Pound the "still point" is much more akin to the Wordsworthian notion of "seeing into the heart of things," although it is far more complex than that. Unlike Stevens, Pound believed in a possible unity of culture and nature, in a union of the historical and the mythical. He could write, for example, in a relatively little known poem called "Religio, or, The Child's Guide to Knowledge":

What is a god?
A god is an eternal state of mind.
What is a faun?
A faun is an elemental creature.
What is a nymph?

> A nymph is an elemental creature.
> When is a god manifest?
> When the states of mind take form.
> When does a man become a god?
> When he enters one of these states of mind.[16]

He could pose such questions directly, and he could answer them directly, without vacillation, something Stevens could never have done. He believed, without question, in the gods. He accepted, without question, the mystical experience.

In *The Spirit of Romance* he wrote, "I believe in a sort of permanent basis in humanity, that is to say, I believe that Greek myth arose when someone having passed through delightful psychic experience tried to communicate it to others and found it necessary to screen himself from persecution." The word "delightful" is weak; we would do better to use the word "ecstatic," which Pound himself uses elsewhere in the same essay to describe the emotion which great art calls forth.

And what is "ecstasy"? "Ecstasy," he says, "is not a whirl of madness of the senses, but a glow arising from the exact nature of perception."[17] In a *Guide to Kulchur* (kulchur and mysticism are linked together, the latter, in part, is a guide to the formation of the former), Pound distinguishes between two kinds of mysticism:

> Two mystic states can be dissociated: the ecstatic-beneficent-and-benevolent, contemplation of the divine love, the divine splendour with goodwill toward others.
> And the bestial, namely the fanatical, the man on fire with God and anxious to stick his snotty nose into other men's business or reprove his neighbor for having a set of tropisms different from that of the fanatic's, or for having the courage to live more greatly and openly.
> The second set of mystic states is manifest in scarcity economists, in repressors etc.
> The first state is a dynamism. It has, time and again, driven men to great living, it has given them courage to go on for decades in the face of public stupidity. It is paradisical and a reward in itself seeking naught further . . . perhaps because a feeling of certitude inheres in the state of feeling itself. The glory of life exists without further proof for this mystic.[18]

In the *Pisan Cantos* Pound experiences the form of mysticism where "the feeling of certitude inheres in the state of feeling itself." In the

Pisan Cantos mysticism, direct perception, periplum, the unexpected moment, paradise, the whole: all these are connected.

Despite the fragmented appearance of these Cantos, the fragments cohere, they spin together. There is a paradox here, if we compare the Stevens poem with the Pound poem. The form of a Stevens poem is well-mannered. All the lines begin politely, properly capitalized, at the left side of the page. Poems are stanzaed and clearly sectioned like oranges. They are carefully crafted, or crated, well-wrought aesthetic urns, they do not spill out "life" in the way that Pound's Cantos or Robert Rauschenberg's combines do. No questionable typographic symbols ($+$, \$, @) or "foreign" foreign languages (Greek, Italian, Latin, to say nothing of Chinese) or disreputable abbreviations (wd/, sd/, s.o.b., and s.h., a.h., and c.s.) intrude. More to the point, the line of a Stevens poem has a clearer narrative direction than do the various Cantos (apart from the fact that the *Pisan Cantos* follow, in time, Pound's stay at the D.T.C.). Stevens built "To an Old Philosopher in Rome," for example, carefully, step by step, block by block; these parts cannot be interchanged, they logically lead to a climax, a kind of epiphany. In the *Pisan Cantos,* on the other hand, bits and pieces of the past, cultural landmarks, snatches of conversations, and memories are tossed together like a salad. But while a syntax of individual parts is missing, the syntax of the whole is not (and we can generalize, the opposite is often true with Stevens). To borrow vocabulary from systems theory, the *Pisan Cantos* are a whole, not a heap. "The excuse for parts of *Ulysses,*" Pound once wrote to Joyce himself, "is the WHOLE of Ulysses; 'serially' it is 'weak.' "[19] The same can be said of the *Pisan Cantos.* It is a grabbag on the level of the individual page, a hodgepodge whose parts, however, form a personal vortex, which is, as Kenner puts it, "a circulation with a still center: a system of energies drawing in whatever comes near." For Pound, Kenner continues, the unwobbling pivot is a transcendental norm.[20]

What is important in the *Pisan Cantos* is just this interpenetration of so many disparate elements. Pound could not sift his life for like images and themes, separating them into so many discrete poems, into clearly labeled bags of corn and oats and wheat. What literary critics do, he could not. To winnow the chaff from one theme (which critics do for the sake of analysis, if not always for the sake of the poem), does more violence to Pound's Cantos than, say, to the poems of Eliot and Stevens. His *Pisan Cantos* are not the Chinese History Cantos or the Adams History Cantos or the Malatesta Cantos. They are his Golden Notebook (to invoke the title of Doris Lessing's well-known novel) where he brings everything together.

I. THE PICARESQUE SAINT

Humanity? is to love men.
Knowledge, is to know men. —Kung[21]

Too much emphasis has been given to the view that the bits and pieces of the *Pisan Cantos* are fastened together by the Poundian act of reminiscence. Noel Stock says bluntly, "The unity of tone is of a man remembering."[22] Hugh Kenner says, "What holds the events of the Pisan sequence together is that they are transacted explicitly within Pound's mind," and this mind is the "mirror of memory."[23] True, in comparison with the preceding Cantos, the tone of elegy and reminiscence is dominant in the Pisan sequence. But the pressure of the present, Pound's fellow prisoners in the D.T.C., the events in the camp—all these are crucial in shaping Pound's experience, and his poem.

Although it is risky to suggest comparison between the novel and poetry (and particularly so after having argued that the narrative line in the *Pisan Cantos* is for all practical purposes nonexistent), still I think one parallel can be quite useful. And that is the similarity that exists between the figure of the picaresque saint which R. W. B. Lewis identifies as central to what he calls second generation fiction[24] and the figure of Pound himself in the *Pisan Cantos*. Lewis proposes, and convincingly so, that while in general twentieth-century (Western) fiction has been concerned, perhaps obsessed, with death in all its forms and meanings (the death of the self, or civilization, of the potency of myth, of God), the first generation of modern writers (Proust, Joyce, Mann) dealt with it by withdrawing into the realm of art, and the second generation (represented for Lewis by Camus, Silone, Moravia, Faulkner, Greene) found "grounds for living *in life itself.*" "Where, in the first generation," Lewis writes, "the image of disintegration was redeemed by the absolute value of art, the sense of nothingness has been transcended, in the second generation, by an agonizing dedication to life.''[25] Both of these solutions, we could say, were adopted by Pound (although not by Stevens), and Pound, for one, would certainly not have found any contradiction between them. Pound straddles, belongs to, two worlds.

But the more important point is this. Lewis describes the picaresque saint as a figure who moves from a sense of loss to a potential gain (a form of conversion), who in great part finds his source of meaning in human companionship and compassion (the sharing of suffering), and who, perhaps most importantly, is both a saint and a sinner. ''The picaresque saint,'' says Lewis, ''tries to hold in balance . . . , by the very contradictions of his character, both the observed truths of contemporary experience and the vital aspiration to transcend them.''[26]

In the work of Ignazio Silone, Lewis points out, the emphasis shifts from politics to charity, and the same is in great part true in Pound's *Pisan Cantos*. The clearest example of the picaresque saint, Lewis argues, is found in Graham Greene's character of the unnamed Mexican priest, the incompetent whiskey-priest who has fathered a child, who is the last practicing Catholic priest in the now totalitarian state, who is an outlaw, who is finally imprisoned with common and not-so-common criminals. It is in prison, says Lewis, that conversion takes place,

> for it is by seeking God and by finding Him in the darkness and stench of prisons, among the sinners and the rats and the rascals, that the whiskey-priest arrives at the richest emotion second generation fiction has to offer: the feeling of companionship, and especially the companionship of the commonly guilty and wretched.[27]

The parallel, rough as it is, between the priest in Greene's *The Power and the Glory* and Pound in the D.T.C. is instructive. But for Pound, it is no fiction, no parable. The emotion of the *Pisan Cantos* is not recollected in Wordsworthian tranquility. The act of writing is not practiced, as it is with Stevens, in a comfortable upstairs study, in a comfortable solitude, late in a quiet night. Pound feared for his life (his death) not at the hands of metaphor or nature, but from the government of men.

During the thirties in Italy, as we can judge from his letters, Pound became increasingly isolated. As he heard from fewer and fewer of his friends, as he worked for fewer magazines, his expression becomes gnarled, his tone shrill and more vituperative. During the war, as we all know, vituperation yielded something more poisonous. That poison, however, is all but missing in the *Pisan Cantos*. Pound had passed, as he puts it, "over Lethe." He had lost his bearings in the world, he was "noman," and had no name, he was in neither Italy nor the United States. He was detained, he was removed and set apart. The cage and the camp were for him ἄχρονος, without time and independent of time. They were also his Mt. Taishan, the mountain where the sage retires to breathe "the process."

Here Pound, picaresque saint, discovers that the rabble, whom he had long held in Shakespearian contempt, was not of a piece:

> Criminals have no intellectual interests?
> "Hey, Snag, wot are the books ov th' bibl'"
> "name 'em, etc.
> "Latin? I studied latin."
>   said the nigger murderer to his cage-mate
> (cdn't be sure which of the two was speaking)
> "c'mon, small fry," sd/ the smaller black lad
>   to the larger.
> "Just playin'" ante mortem no scortum
> (that's progress, me yr'" se/call it progress/).
>
>   [LXXVI]

"Dawley," "Tom," "Whiteside," and "Romano Ramona," and "Scott," "Salazar," and "Washington," and "Benin," especially "Benin"—these names are just as important to Pound as "William B.Y.," "Dr. Williams," and "dear H.J. (Mr. James, Henry)," or "Demeter" and "Cythera" or any of those which form any of the other countless categories of names. With these people Pound found companionship. From them he received charity, perhaps learned charity. As he relates in the opening Canto:

> and Mr Edwards superb green and brown
>   in ward No 4 a jacent benignity,

> of the Baluba mask: "doan you tell no one
>> I made you that table"
>>> methenamine eases the urine
>> and the greatest is charity
> to be found among those who have not observed
>>> regulations.
>>>>>> [LXXIV]

And a few pages later he writes, "Filial, fraternal affection is the root of humaneness" (LXXIV).

In the *Pisan Cantos* Pound also fulfills another dimension of the picaresque saint. He confesses, "J'ai eu pitié des autres/probablement pas assez, and at moments that suited my own convenience" (LXXVI). He admits, "There can be honesty of mind/without overwhelming talent" (LXXX). He learns that no one "who has passed a month in the death cells/[can] believe in capital punishment" (LXXXIII). He vows that "nothing matters but the quality/of the affection" (LXXVI). He affirms, "Amo ergo sum" (LXXX), and in so doing rejects the dominant tradition of dualism, the unhealthy bias toward the "objective" and the "scientific," in Western thought since the Greeks and certainly since Descartes.[28]

"Senesco sed amo" (LXXX): This is both a personal revelation and a declaration as to how one should live. Pound chooses, in the words of Castaneda, a path with a heart.[29] In these Cantos we see him honoring the dead in order to live by that rule. It is, in other words, not so much out of nostalgia as out of a desire to pay homage to what he has loved in his life that Pound composes his hymn to the dead. He recites the litany of restaurants and cafes ("Dieudonné," "La Rupé," and "Dullier") and the litany of artists of his generation ("Jepson" and "Newbolt" and others: "Lordly men are to earth o'ergiven" [LXXIV]).

As a result of this, which is first and foremost an act of love, Pound plots the curve of his own past. Periplum: I am getting old but I love. He establishes his own existence. He makes the Cantos his archives. He gives us (as he certainly could never resist doing, but here the spirit is not Poundian didactic imperative) a bibliography, an inventory of an important part of the twentieth-century past. The bibliography: like the journal, it too has become an important form in the seventies, providing a thread to follow through the information explosion (think of Ihab Hassan and his paracriticism, of the *Whole Earth Catalogue* and its countless imitators, of Norman O. Brown's work). Pound was thinking, we can suppose, not only of pinpointing a specific landscape for himself (with accurate dates and names and places, this no Wallace Stevens landscape of the mind), but of the future "archeologist" and historian as well who would want just those objects as *markers,* as raw data. Here again the appropriate parallel in the visual (and plastic) arts is with Rauschenberg, whose work ("combines") of the fifties not only represents a whole (a state of mind, perhaps) but includes, in fact, the object—object*s*—thus transforming "life" into "art" only by shifting these objects from one context to another (a new text), by leaving them otherwise to stand primary, as fact. In the *Pisan Cantos* fragments of memory are, like Rauschenberg's objects, as hard and as durable and as lasting as the stone carvings of the Santa Maria dei Miracoli, which Pound so highly cherished. They confer a kind of benediction:

> and as for the solidity of the white oxen in all this
> perhaps only Dr Williams (Bill Carlos)
> will understand its importance,
> its benediction. He wd/ have put in the cart.
>
> [LXXVIII]

II. THE RESACRALIZATION OF THE LANDSCAPE
THE SPIRIT OF ROMANCE

The celestial and earthly process pervades and is substantial; it is on high and gives light, it comprehends the light and endures.

—Confucius[30]

Pound, with his monetary history of the West, is the Milton Friedman of American poetry. Pound, with his *Guide to Kulchur,* his support of Mussolini, and his life-long devotion to the classics, wherever he found them, is the supreme poet of culture, both pragmatic and imaginative, among America's great Modernists. And so it is with some surprise, a pleasant surprise, that Pound ("I detest the country"[31]) turns to the "green world" in the *Pisan Cantos.* Pound, the poet of culture, becomes the poet of nature as well. So much so, in fact, that at several points these Cantos resemble the greater Romantic lyric of the English Romantics.

If we adopt the Confucian model of man's development, we see that Pound, having looked into his own heart, was now able to turn to the larger world beyond, to be part of the "process." At one with himself, he could now be one with the mysteries of the world. One of the Confucian passages that he translated at the D.T.C. describes this very shift in perspective:

> He who possesses this sincerity does not lull himself to somnolence perfecting himself with egocentric aim, but he has a further efficiency in perfecting something outside himself.
> Fulfilling himself he attains full manhood, perfecting things outside himself he attains knowledge.
> The inborn nature begets this activity naturally, this looking straight into oneself and thence acting. These two activities constitute the process which unites outer and inner, object and subject, and thence constitutes a harmony with the seasons of earth and heaven.[32]

For Pound the goal now becomes the union of inner and outer, and the outer is the entire system of the natural world, "the seasons of earth and heaven," and not, as it is for Stevens, the single object, the "thing itself."

For Pound the natural landscape offered permanence and continuity. He believed that it is nature that ultimately remains (today, of course, in our artificial landscape of freeways and state camping grounds, we know that nature's permanence is threatened). He believed that the beauty of nature could be found everywhere, and that this beauty could save him; as he remarks throughout the *Pisan Cantos,* "the clouds near to Pisa/are as good as any in Italy" (LXXVI). But more importantly, Pound understood man's essential dependence upon the land, his origins in the land: "man, earth : two halves of the tally" (LXXXII). He called upon the natural world for protection ("o lynx, guard my vineyard" [LXXIX]). In the D.T.C. it was nature—the green lizard, the butterfly, the wasp building her nest, the ant's forefoot—which sustained him, and more, fulfilled him:

° in about 1/2 a day she has made her adobe
(la vespa) the tiny mud-flask
and that day I wrote no further.

[LXXXIII]

The quiet miracle of the wasp constructing an object of ''culture'' (the adobe) in and out of the ''natural'' (the mud) eases the need for Pound to make his own shelter through the act of writing; the natural and the cultural, he realizes as witness to this event, can be, could be, are, not separate and distinct, but two aspects of the same reality.

When man is concerned only with man, Pound wrote in *The Spirit of Romance,* he ''forgets the whole and the flowing.''[33] Never a humanist, Pound looked to the green world for centering and balancing. The world, he knew, was not man's world, but rather man was part of the world:

The ant's a centaur in his dragon world.
Pull down thy vanity, it is not man
Made courage, or made order, or made grace,
Pull down thy vanity, I say pull down.
Learn of the green world what can be thy place
In scaled invention or true artistry,
Pull down thy vanity,
Paquin pull down!
The green casque has outdone your elegance.

[LXXXI]

But Pound's view of the green world is more profound and more magical and more visionary than this. ''Wisdom lies next thee, / simply, past metaphor,'' he writes of Terra (LXXXII); and ''Arum vult nemus'' (LXXVIII): the grove needs an altar. It is just this altar which he discovers (or better, *gives*) in the *Pisan Cantos.* What is an altar? An icon, a cultural artifact, and culture, Pound believed, must again be formed and called upon to serve nature. Among other things (and he himself is included), what he offers to the green world, what he makes new, is the mythology of Greece and Rome. And this is a lesson profoundly important for our time. Since the seventeenth century, the emphasis of Western science on ''objectivity'' has worked to sever man from nature, allowed man to regard nature as dead, as a mere thing and a lifeless object, and thus sanctioned the rape of the earth. The emphasis on methodology, reason, and logic in the wake of Descartes and Bacon has discredited other forms of awareness, among them, the intuitive and the imaginative.

As Roszak points out, the psychological mode is different in the two cases:

> Objectivity involves a breaking off of personal contact between observer and observed; there is an act of psychic contradiction back and away from what is studied for the sake of a sharp, undistracted focus. In contrast, moral unselfishness means to identify with the other, to reach out and embrace and feel with. Far from being a contraction of the self, here we have expansion, a profoundly personal activity of the soul. At its warmest and more complete, this expansive relationship of self to other becomes love, and issues forth gracefully in compassion, sacrifice, magnanimity. And *these,* not any sort of rational calibration or intellectual precision, are the secret of peace and joyous community. These alone provide a balance to the murdering furies of the political arena.[34]

In the first case, there is a distancing of the self from the other; the relationship is clinical and cold, and the "other" is reduced to the status of the object. In the second, the self and the other move toward each other; the relationship is ethical and "warm." As Roszak traces the curve of Western intellectual history, he observes that with the triumph of the attitude of objectivity, there is a progressive "thickening of the world's substance,"[35] ending in the totally desacralized world of the twentieth century. "What becomes of a world purged of its sacramental capacities?" he asks. "It dies the death of the spirit," he answers, and concludes that "beauty cut loose of its sacramental base is a decadent pleasure and a vulnerable one."[36] For a solution to our problem Roszak turns to the English Romantics for a politics of eternity, but he could have turned to Pound as well. For Pound too believed that we "have lost the radiant world where one thought cuts through another with clean edges, a world of moving energies."[37]

Kenner accuses Pound of indulging in several of the early Cantos in "a kaleidoscope of fancies, visions, glimpses, flickering wonders that merge into postwar reality."[38] In the *Pisan Cantos* there are also visions and glimpses and flickering wonders but here it is no indulgence. For Pound, the earth is feminine, the earth is mother, and it is also alive with her goddesses. The natural and the mythical merge, become interchangeable, identical. The natural and the mythological here are different aspects of the same reality; the name of the one calls the other. Metaphor collapses to unity, identity; identity resonates with meaning and metaphor. The wind is part of the process, the wind is Zephyrus, Zephyrus is thus part of the process. Tellus is the divinity of earth, nature is another name for divinity. The familiar landscape is populated with goddesses transformed, tree nymphs, the hamadryas, who were changed into poplar trees while mourning their brother Phaethon: the nymph and the tree are one. The earth is both mother and lover, she is "χθόνια γεα, Μήτηρ" and Demeter, the goddess of fruitfulness and harvest:

> bel seno (in rimas escarsas, vide sopra)
> 2 mountains with the Arno, I suppose, flowing between
> them so kissed the earth after sleeping on concrete
>
> bel seno Δημήτηρ copulatrix
>   thy furrow.
>
>   [LXXVII]

This passage, and the *Pisan Cantos* as a whole, is particularly interesting because it illustrates how Pound has merged the two paths to wholeness—the ascetic and the chivalric—which he had outlined many years earlier in *The Spirit of Romance*. In that book he had championed the chivalric path (exemplified by the troubadour who seeks wholeness through sex, through union with his opposite, woman) rather than that of the ascetic (exemplified by the monk who, Pound had said dryly, achieved wholeness, "at infinite trouble and expense," through contemplation).[39] Here, in Pisa, through the force of a Coleridgean imagination, he keeps the path of the troubadour open (Stevens, of course, had never recognized its existence, and Williams never really had another) while at the same time following the contemplative path of the ascetic. The system is complete; in the *Pisan Cantos* Pound practices a kind of ecology of ideas. The metaphor is organic; mind works on matter. His consciousness is what he called in *The Spirit of Romance*, "germinal":

Their thoughts [those who possess a "germinal" consciousness] are in them as the thought of the tree is in the seed, or in the grass, or the grain, or the blossom. And these minds are the more poetic, and they affect mind about them, and transmute it as the seed the earth. And this latter sort of mind is close on the vital universe; and the strength of the Greek beauty rests in this, that it is ever at the interpretation of this vital universe, by its signs of gods and godly attendants and oreads.[40]

In the *Pisan Cantos* the act of contemplation (or better, state of contemplation) cannot be separated from the power of woman, the feminine; the one (each one) makes the other possible. We remember that of the three modes of thought—cognition, meditation, and contemplation—that Pound had identified, the last was of the highest order, its truth verifiable by experience. "In the first," he wrote in *Guide to Kulchur*, "the mind flits aimlessly about the object, in the second it circles about it in a methodical manner, in the third it is unified with the object."[41] Unified with the object: woman.

But the earth is for Pound more than his lover, she is his savior. Pound loses himself in order to gain his self, a new self:

> man, earth : two halves of the tally
> but I will come out of this knowing no one
> neither they me
> >   connubium terrae   ἔφατα πόσις ἐμός
> >   ΧΘΟΝΙΟΣ, mysterium
> fluid ΧΘΟΝΟΣ o'erflowed me
>   lay in the fluid ΧΘΟΝΟΣ
> >   that lie
> under the air's solidity
> >   drunk with 'ΙΧΩΡ of ΧΘΟΝΙΟΣ
> >   fluid ΧΘΟΝΟΣ, strong as the undertow
> >   of the wave receding
> >   [LXXXII]

Death by water? yes, but as in Eliot's "The Waste Land," the water is a primal fluid, it returns one to the source. This is one of the reasons, we can suppose, that the sage (as Confucius, and after him, Pound, observed) is associated with water. "The humane man has amity with the hills," writes Pound in Canto LXXIII, and he is that humane man. But the "sage / delighteth in water," and he is that too.

The earth for Pound is magical and alive with power. And in the *Pisan Cantos* he is able, finally, to draw on this power. He becomes a shaman; the eucalyptus pip and the texts of Confucius are his allies. Know thyself: that was the first step, to recognize and confess his lack of compassion for others, to open his heart. The second step was to honor and embrace a power larger than his, an inhuman power, the other world. The third step is more aptly termed a condition, a state of mind. It is repeated throughout the *Pisan Cantos:*

> "Non combaattere" said Giovanna,
> meaning: don't work so hard.
>
> [LXXVI]

Meaning, as Mencius had instructed: "Let not the mind forget its work, but let there be no assisting the growth of nature." Meaning, the ease of mind, which Stevens, we remember, also seeks in his last book of poems. It is that ease of mind, the arrest of the Western habit of categorizing and dividing, that allows the unexpected to happen, that permits multiplication of possibilities. And the unexpected is—what? It is itself that inexplicable state of mind ("States of mind are inexplicable to us." [LXXVI]) where different worlds, alternative realities, interpass and penetrate. Pound has learned how to call up the spirits of both realms—the natural and the mythical—when he needs them, and this we must take literally, as he did.

In one of the most lyrical passages in the *Pisan Cantos* he calls upon the lynx not only to protect his vines but to keep Dionysus running in his veins.[42] As we see in the closing lines of Canto LXXIX, the lynx and Aphrodite are two forms of the same power; he can pass from one to the other without visible (logical) transition:

> O lynx guard my vineyard
> As the grape swells under vine leaf
>
> This Goddess was born of sea-foam
> She is lighter than air under Hesperus
>   δεινὰ εἶ, Κύθηρα
> terrible in resistance
>   Κόρη καὶ Δήλια καὶ Μαῖα
> trine as praeludio

Κύπρις 'Αφρόδιτη
a petal lighter than sea-foam
Κύθηρα
aram
nemus
vult
O puma, sacred to Hermes, Cimbica servant of Helios.

[LXXIX]

Aphrodite is only one of the many goddesses he summons. The names
are for him charms. This he had asserted long before. In *The Spirit of
Romance* he had observed that "alchemy and mystical philosophy
interpenetrate each other, and that feminine names were used as
charms or equations in alchemy"; and that furthermore, "anyone who
has in any degree the faculty of vision will know that the so-called
personifications are real and not artificial."[43]

Knowing that such things are real and not just figures of speech—
this is the spirit of romance. The names and the names behind the
names flood these Cantos: Persephone and Pallas Athena and Cytherea
and Maya and Aphrodite and the Heliads and Cassandra. In Canto
LXXXI the goddess goes unnamed but her existence is no less concrete
for that:

Ed ascoltando al leggier mormorio
there came new subtlety of eyes into my tent,
whether of spirit or hypostasis,
but what the blindfold hides
or at carneval
nor any pair showed anger
Saw but the eyes and stance between the eyes,
colour, diastasis,
careless or unaware it had not the
whole tent's room
nor was place for full Εἰδώς
interpass, penetrate
casting but shade beyond the other lights
sky's clear

> night's sea
> green of the mountain pool
> shone from the unmasked eyes in half-mask's space.
>
> [LXXXI]

The eyes of the goddess(es) enter his tent; no metaphor: "I assert," he had said in *Guide to Kulchur,* "that the Gods exist."[44] Invisible, they yet cast shadows; translucent, they show him the "clear" and "green" landscape of the natural world.

This point is not Ειδὼς, the full revelation, but in the last of the *Pisan Cantos* there is a final transference. Those eyes become his eyes, he sees the magical/natural world with the eyes of that world. Recall the first of the *Pisan Cantos* where Pound speaks of the eye containing nature, but only in simile; when that was achieved it would be time to go:

> night green of his pupil, as grape flesh and sea wave
> undying luminous and translucent
>
> Est consummatum, Ite.
>
> [LXXIV]

And in the next to the last Canto, in pellucid, simple lines that are almost overlooked, Pound can write:

> A fat moon rises lop-sided over the mountain
> The eyes, this time my world,
>   But pass and look *from* mine
>   between my lids
>   sea, sky, and pool
>   alternate
>   pool, sky, sea.
>
> [LXXXIII]

This is not the empyrean of pure light, the mystic ecstasy which Dante felt looking at Beatrice (which Pound took as a model), but it is a union with the magical other. This is Pound's point of stillness and peace. Now, "in the drenched tent there is quiet / sered eyes are at rest":

or

as he was standing below the altars
of the spirits of rain.

[LXXXIII]

In the *Pisan Cantos* Pound succeeds in resacralizing the landscape for
us as well as himself, and "out of all this beauty," even in Pisa, in
spite of Pisa, because of Pisa, "something," he believes, "must
come" (LXXIV).

III. ETHNO-UTOPIA

My *Paradiso* will have no St Dominic or Augustine, but it will be a
Paradiso just the same, moving toward final coherence. I'm getting at
the building of the City, that whole tradition. Augustine, he don't
amount to a great deal. —Pound, 1953[45]

In the *Pisan Cantos* the reinvestment (as in "religious vestments")
of the landscape with a living, sexual dimension, or to put it another
way, the reunion of the natural with the magical and mythological (the
super-natural) is analogous to the equally important fusion of the historical with the mythical. As William Irwin Thompson has deftly
pointed out, myth is the detritus of history.[46] Just as the goddesses exist
and are to be believed, so myth contains truths which are not merely
metaphorical but real, historical. It was Pound, not Eliot, who understood what the discoveries in the then-new field of anthropology
meant. Eliot accepted the parables of Western culture (the journey to
the Perilous Chapel to see the Fisher-King) as convenient metaphor to
point to the contemporary Western wasteland. But Pound knew, as he
wrote in the *Pisan Cantos,* that Homer had been a medic, that that
ancient journey had been based on rock-real experience. And if that
were so, then he could conclude that the dreams of utopian cities and
civilizations could also have been based on the historical record.

In the *Pisan Cantos* Pound resacralizes the landscape, and her goddesses bring him peace. Only with such a personal equilibrium, Confucius had taught, could a man bring amelioration to the state. And
for Pound, if those luminous eyes deliver peace, it is the city which
gives inspiration. If the first represents the feminine principle of acceptance and union, the second does not so much represent the masculine

principle of action (the hero constructing his civilization's meaning in monument), as it incorporates the two. In the *Pisan Cantos* Pound, like Confucius, his master and ally, is a sage, a wise old man. It is his mission to reinvent the imaginary city, to dream the city anew, to resurrect an ideal. Years before, he had asked in his *Guide to Kulchur* if a modern Eleusis was "possible in the wilds of a man's mind only."[47] In the *Pisan Cantos* he answers yes.

Of the four great American Moderns, Pound was the only poet to believe in what we now call ethnopoetics—the coupling of anthropology and poetry, the opening up of other, nonwestern cultural traditions—both as method and metaphor.[48] In the *Pisan Cantos* Pound was fighting not only for his own personal survival, but for the survival of the Western world as well. For survival, he knew that the industrial West had to turn to cultures which were based on values other than that of profit, and ideals other than that of the economy of abundance with its concomitant disposable and interchangeable objects, its scorn of both masterpiece and craft. He turned to Provence and to Greece, but more significantly he turned to China, and Africa, and even, occasionally, to the American Algonquin.

Thus, to dwell on Pound as exile, as directing his major effort toward breaking the English tradition, represented by the pentameter, is to belittle his achievement. Pound was not so much an exile as he was a citizen of the world. He had defended himself against that charge; as he had written to Harriet Monroe in 1914, "Are you going to call people foreigners the minute they care enough about their art to travel in order to perfect it."[49] Pound did believe in kulchur, in what he called a "vortex," in what his favorite anthropologist, Froebenius, called "paideuma," but he was not foolish enough, fortunately he was not provincial enough, to confuse this with nationality and the nation-state.

In the *Pisan Cantos*, achieving wholeness, attaining that point which I have called the still point, has multiple meanings. It not only refers to the personal state of peace which Pound experiences and which is, importantly, both psychological and social; these two aspects are interrelated by the process of his integrating himself into the human ("criminal") community, and here the relationship of the self to the social unit is an ethical one. But, the still point also refers to the quiet union of Pound with the natural world ("and that day I wrote no further" [LXXXIII]), and here the relationship of the self to the other is a sacramental one. And the still point also refers to that ideal of human civilization which Pound reincarnates for himself, in both his heart and his mind, and for us in the living text of the poem. Here the relationship of the self to the ideal is a creative one.

While Pound does not provide us with a blueprint for utopia, we can conclude that for him the perfect society would be a completely integrated "pure" culture which drew on its own traditions for its foundation, as he presumably believed China had. Having lost this, the commercial West (dating from the invention of the institution of banking), he believed, had no other choice but to embrace cultural pluralism. This presents us with a problem, for the goal and the method are contradictory. In the *Pisan Cantos,* Pound is interested above all in opening up and bringing together as many different domains as possible—the domain of affection, the domain of the magical, the domain of alternative traditions—and yet the ultimate ideal is that of a closed and static society. Although this contradiction cannot be resolved in the real and historical world (history implies change, change in great part comes from the collision of cultures), Pound attempts to resolve it through art.

"To build the city of Dioce whose terraces are the colours of stars" (LXXIV), a heavenly city on earth, that is the goal. The city of Dioce was Persian but the model Pound appeals to is African:

> 4 times was the city rebuilded, Hooo Fasa
>   Gassir, Hooo Fasa   dell' Italia tradita
> now in the mind indestructible, Gassir, Hooo Fasa,
> With the four giants at the four corners
> and four gates mid-wall Hooo Fasa
> and a terrace the colour of stars.

> [LXXIV]

The promise of Gassir's city offers a promise to Italy:

> I believe in the resurrection of Italy
>   4 times to the song of Gassir
>   now in the mind indestructible.

> [LXXIV]

Pound is not here resurrecting myth (Gassir and the African city) so as to make history possible (the triumph of Italy). Rather he is resurrecting history so as to make the myth of Italy's future possible. The act is an imaginative one, a pure one:

> funge la purezza,
> and that certain images be formed in the mind
> to remain there
> *formato locho.*
>
> [LXXIV]

This is another way of saying that the word must be made perfect (''cheng ming''), that language (and literature) constitute the building blocks of civilization. And as the feminine principle is at the root of nature, so it is at the base of the legend of Gassir's lute, for Wagadu is woman. It is woman that man must find again, as we see in the following account of the legend, which, of course, Pound was familiar with:

> Four times Wagadu stood there in all her splendour, four times Wagadu disappeared and was lost to human sight: once through vanity, once through falsehood, once through greed, and once through dissension. Four times Wagadu changed her name. First she was called Dierra, then Agada, then Ganna, then Silla. Four times she turned her face. Once to the north, once to the west, once to the east, and once to the south. For Wagadu, whenever men have seen her, has always had four gates: one to the north, one to the west, one to the east, and one to the south. These are the directions whence the strength of Wagadu comes, the strength in which she endures no matter whether she be built of stone, wood, or earth, or lives but as a shadow in the mind and longing of her children. For really, Wagadu is not of stone, not of wood, not of earth. Wagadu is the strength which lives in the hearts of men and is sometimes visible because eyes see her and ears hear the clash of swords and ring of shields, and is sometimes invisible because the indomitability of men has overtired her, so that she sleeps. Sleep came to Wagadu for the first time through vanity, for the second time through falsehood, for the third time through greed, and for the fourth time through dissension. Should Wagadu ever be found for the fifth time, she will live again, so forcefully that vanity, falsehood, greed and dissension will never be able to harm her.
> Hooh! Dierra, Agada, Ganna, Silla! Hooh! Fasa![50]

The promise: if found a fifth time, Wagadu "will never be lost again."
Deliverance: in the *Pisan Cantos* the song is "now in the mind indestructible" (LXXIV).

What did Pound believe in, Eliot has asked. "I believe," he answered, "the *Ta Hio*."[51] What Confucius offered him was a "respon-
sible" way of life: Confucius thinks, as Pound put it, "for the whole
social order," something which both Greek and Christian thought did
not do.[52] Thus for Pound poetry is tied to "the whole social order," to
politics and to economics and to ethics, and the link is a direct, not an
indirect, one; as he wrote, for example, to René Taupin in 1928, "Je
viens de donner un noveau version du *Ta Hio* de Confucius, parce que
j'y trouve des formulations d'idées qui me paraissent utile pour
civiliser l'Amérique (tentatif)."[53] This belief that the province of
poetry is "the whole social order" is Pound's great strength, his source
of optimism, and one of his major contributions. We have him to thank
for his persistent affirmation throughout the first half of the twentieth
century, a period in Western history preoccupied with its "heap of
broken images," of the possibility of a "new sacred book of the arts,"
as Yeats called it. A sacred book which would heal the splits in culture,
remove, in effect, the banks from the position of power and place the
artists in the position of authority.

Pound, all his life, assumed a role of leadership and wrote from a
position of confidence and authority. His tone is vigorous and bracing
as well as inspiring. His style embodies that kind of idea which, as he
describes it, is "intended to 'go into action', or to guide action and
serve us as rules (and/or) measures of conduct." What is the other kind
of idea? It is that which exists and/or is, Pound says, "discussed in a
species of vacuum," which is as it were a toy "of the intellect."[54] It
is to this second category of ideas that we could assign Stevens' notion
of a supreme fiction, and the contrast between his idea of a supreme
fiction and Pound's hopes and beliefs is a telling one.

For Stevens, Western culture had broken and could not be made
new. The only strategy was to hold two opposing and irreconcilable
ideas in the mind at once. "The final belief," Stevens had written, "is
to believe in a fiction, which you know to be a fiction, there being

nothing else.''[55] The strategy was, in other words, solely an individual matter and could not, did not, include society, the community. But for Pound the "fiction" (whether it was Wagadu or the goddesses or the companionship of men) was not a fiction but real. And the "fiction" involved not just the healing (the state of wholeness) of the individual but the dream of an integrated, healthy social order and an harmonious relationship between these two systems (man and society) and that of the cosmos as well, where the cosmos is equivalent to the mysteries. "Our time," Pound had written, "has overshadowed the mysteries by an overemphasis on the individual.''[56]

The "unwobbling pivot" is not only the metaphor for, but also the actual point of, balance of all these systems both together and separately. "The master(man)finds the center and does not waver," Pound translated Confucius, and that "axis in the center is the great root of the universe.''[57] The wisdom of the *Pisan Cantos* is the wisdom of one wise old man, Pound, who himself understands that we must listen to the wisdom of the old, internalize the old, and not fall prey to the tradition of the new (which is an economics of consumption and waste on all levels). "Philosophy is not for young men" (LXXIV), Pound wrote early in the *Pisan Cantos*. This is another way of saying that wisdom is reserved for, is the privilege of, the old. And as Simone de Beauvoir points out, the important thing to understand is that the status of the old is "never *won* but always *granted*.''[58]

1. Confucius, *The Great Digest, The Unwobbling Pivot, The Analects,* trans. Ezra Pound (New York: New Directions, 1951), pp. 167–69.

2. Noel Stock, *Reading the Cantos: The Study of Meaning in Ezra Pound* (London: Routledge & Kegan Paul, 1967), p. 87.

3. Guy Davenport, "Persephone's Ezra," in *New Approaches to Ezra Pound,* ed. Eva Hesse (London: Faber and Faber, 1969), pp. 145–73.

4. Ezra Pound, *Guide to Kulchur* (New York: New Directions, 1952), p. 196.

5. Letter from Ezra Pound to Homer L. Pound, April 11, 1927, in *Selected Letters of Ezra Pound: 1907–1941,* ed. D. D. Paige (New York: New Directions, 1971), p. 219.

6. *The Great Digest, The Unwobbling Pivot, The Analects,* p. 169.

7. *Selected Letters of Ezra Pound,* p. 210.

8. Hugh Kenner, *The Pound Era* (Berkeley: University of California Press, 1971), p. 33. Kenner's discussion of the *Pisan Cantos,* it goes without saying, is the best to date.

9. Ezra Pound, *The Spirit of Romance* (New York: New Directions, 1952), p. 153.

10. "Note" to Harry Crosby's *Torchbearer* (1931), reprinted in *Alcheringa,* no. 5 (Spring-Summer 1973), 92.

11. Ezra Pound, *Gaudier-Brzeska: A Memoir* (New York: New Directions, 1960), p. 86.

12. *The Pound Era,* p. 178.

13. Ezra Pound, *Literary Essays of Ezra Pound,* ed. T. S. Eliot (New York: New Directions, 1968), p. 3.

14. *Literary Essays of Ezra Pound,* p. 4.

15. See Hugh Kenner's discussion of the difference between the "glimpse" and the "vision" in *The Pound Era,* pp. 69–72, 173–91.

16. Ezra Pound, *Pavannes & Divagations* (New York: Alfred A. Knopf, 1918).

17. *The Spirit of Romance,* pp. 92, 91.

18. *Guide to Kulchur,* pp. 223–24.

19. *Selected Letters of Ezra Pound,* p. 151.

20. *The Pound Era,* pp. 239, 455.

21. Quoted in *Guide to Kulchur,* p. 18.

22. Stock, *Reading the Cantos,* p. 78.

23. "The Broken Mirrors and the Mirror of Memory," in *Motive and Method in "The Cantos" of Ezra Pound,* ed. Lewis Leary (New York: Columbia University Press, 1954), pp. 25–32.

24. R. W. B. Lewis, *The Picaresque Saint: Representative Figures in Contemporary Fiction* (Philadelphia: J. B. Lippincott, 1959).

25. *The Picaresque Saint,* p. 27.

26. *The Picaresque Saint,* p. 31.

27. *The Picaresque Saint,* p. 30.

28. As Pound wrote in a letter to Katue Kitasono on November 15, 1940 (*Selected Letters of Ezra Pound,* p. 347): "Ideogram is essential to the exposition of certain kinds of thought. Greek philosophy was mostly a mere splitting, an impoverishment of understanding, though it ultimately led to development of particular sciences."

29. See the "novels" of Carlos Castaneda.

30. *The Great Digest, The Unwobbling Pivot, The Analects,* p. 179.

31. Letter to Isabel W. Pound, November 1913, in *Selected Letters of Ezra Pound,* p. 25.

32. *The Great Digest, The Unwobbling Pivot, The Analects,* p. 179.

33. *The Spirit of Romance,* p. 93.

34. Theodore Roszak, *Where the Wasteland Ends: Politics and Transcendence in Post-Industrial Society* (Garden City, N.Y.: Doubleday, 1973), p. 244.

35. *Where the Wasteland Ends,* p. 126.

36. *Where the Wasteland Ends,* p. 127.

37. *Literary Essays of Ezra Pound,* p. 154.

38. *The Pound Era,* p. 418.

39. *The Spirit of Romance,* p. 94.

40. *The Spirit of Romance,* pp. 92–93.

41. *The Guide to Kulchur,* p. 77.

42. This is a gesture from the fourth dimension: "The fourth; the dimension of stillness. / And the power over wild beasts" (XLIX).

43. *The Spirit of Romance,* pp. 106, 126.

44. *Guide to Kulchur,* p. 77.

45. Interview at St. Elizabeth Hospital, July 17, 1953; quoted by Guy Davenport, "Pound and Frobenius," in *Motive and Method in the Cantos of Ezra Pound,* p. 52.

46. *Passages about Earth: An Exploration of the New Planetary Culture* (New York: Harper and Row, 1973), pp. 119–49.

47. *Guide to Kulchur,* p. 294.

48. Jerome Rothenberg, whose influential anthology *Technicians of the Sacred: A Range of Poetries from Africa, America, Asia, and Oceania* (Garden City, N.Y.: Doubleday, 1968) first brought into sharp focus the likeness of contemporary oral poetry to "primitive" poetries, has repeatedly affirmed the continuities of the oral tradition, and each time he has emphasized (1) that the golden spool (as André Breton called it) has spun a thread traversing Pound's idea of the "image," (2) his regard for Worringer's account of the primitive in art, and (3) his restoration of the oral impulse as the ground of poetry. The term "ethnopoetics" was coined by Rothenberg and Dennis Tedlock in the first number of the journal *Alcheringa* (Fall 1970), which they coedited; in that issue they quote from Ezra Pound's *Guide to Kulchur* (p. 5). In his 1973 interview with William Spanos published in the Spring 1975 issue of *Boundary 2* (the entire issue is devoted to contemporary oral poetry), Rothenberg again pays homage to Pound's work, as well as that of Stein, Williams, Cummings, Duchamp, the Dadaists, the Surrealists, the Objectivists, and so on, as "germinal" for his own generation, but regrets Pound's "reluctance to follow through on the implications of his own poetic practice" (p. 521). But Rothenberg's reservations mostly center on the implications and practice of New Criticism, which has been based on the Eliot-Pound nexus in literary criticism.

49. *Selected Letters of Ezra Pound,* p. 37.

50. Leo Frobenius and Douglas C. Fox, *African Genesis* (London: Faber and Faber, 1938), pp. 109–10.

51. *Literary Essays of Ezra Pound,* p. 86.

52. *Guide to Kulchur,* p. 29.

53. *Selected Letters of Ezra Pound,* p. 217.

54. *Guide to Kulchur,* p. 299.

55. Wallace Stevens, *Opus Posthumous* (New York: Alfred A. Knopf, 1966), p. 63.

56. *Guide to Kulchur,* p. 299.

57. *The Great Digest, The Unwobbling Pivot, The Analects,* p. 103.

58. *The Coming of Age,* p. 129.

4

WALLACE STEVENS AND *THE ROCK*

Not Ideas about Nobility
but the Thing Itself

Union of the weakest develops strength
Not wisdom. Can all men, together, avenge
One of the leaves that have fallen in autumn?
But the wise man avenges by building his city in snow.

But the wise man avenges by building his city in snow. This is how Stevens concludes "Like Decorations in a Nigger Cemetery," the longest piece in *Ideas of Order* (1936), his second collection of poems. An icy pronouncement, this declaration suggests the shape and strategy of the hero that emerges eighteen years later in Stevens' last book of poems, *The Rock*.[1] As prophecy, these lines promise more than Stevens could ever deliver or later desired: that the master builder construct a citadel of belief for the modern age. This would have been a supreme fiction, an act of defiant will. But what the hero could not do for Western culture, Stevens learned in the years between *Ideas of Order* and *The Rock,* a man could do for himself in a different mood, a variant key. It comes to this: the wise man faces mortality, the human condition (or what is perhaps the same thing for Stevens, the death of belief), on its own ground: alone, old, he makes his home in the wasteland, in winter, in the extreme of the unknown. By facing death and living within it, not fighting it, the hero, the "impossible possible philosophers' man," develops what in old age Stevens understood as wisdom. Not power, but an acceptance of the possibility of congruence between a man's meditative life and the inhuman meditation of the world ("the leaves that have fallen in autumn"). The hero of *The Rock*—and for the abstract-minded Stevens this is the highest achievement—is no longer a theoretical construct or more than human. He is a man who does not take possession of the world by intellectual storm, the act of the mind, but rather lives in harmony with it.

If the concluding lines of "Like Decorations in a Nigger Cemetery" point toward what Stevens achieves in his last book of poems, they also reveal what he could never accept. Unlike Eliot, Pound, or Williams, Stevens was never passionately concerned with the quest for community. In the *Pisan Cantos,* the union of the weakest—the social bond forged by imprisonment—does foster wisdom. But for Pound, wisdom entails affection and humility, personal virtues, ultimately social virtues, which Stevens never believed essential to the hero. Of the four Moderns considered here, Stevens was the only one who never thought in terms of an ideal society or a utopia, but only in terms of *a* hero, *the* hero, the solitary mind. Only the Stevens hero stands alone and apart. Stevens posed questions of culture, certainly, but in epistemological, not political or social, terms. And it is perhaps as a result of this that we find his work, so elegant, so perfect, so deeply satisfying, yet so often chilly and curiously removed from the problems of twentieth-century industrial society. Because Stevens basically ignored such questions, in this chapter I look more closely at the individual poems. In order to put the achievement of *The Rock* in perspective, I begin by looking at Stevens' earlier versions of the hero and then turn to his treatment of death in earlier poems.

I. CONCEPT ART: ABSTRACTION AS HERO

The major abstraction is the idea of man
And major man is its exponent, abler
In the abstract than in his singular,

More fecund as principle than particle
　　　　　　　"Notes Toward a Supreme Fiction"

As we have seen in the last lines of "Like Decorations in a Nigger Cemetery," at that point in his life Stevens wished to taunt death and the "search for a tranquil belief" called for earlier in the poem. This contradiction in the poem is contained within its last line. We expect it to read: "The wise man builds his city in snow," and in our misreading we uncover the tension between the figure of the hero as youthful avenger and Stevens' well-kept, persistent desire for the ascetic wisdom of tranquility. This contradiction haunts much of Stevens' work until *The Rock.*

We understand, only in retrospect possibly, that his hero was always too young, too vigorously grandiose, too abstract, or too barbarous for Stevens' basically peaceful purposes. The problem was this. He recognized, as we all know too well (this has become a banality of criticism, a truth difficult to revive), that we live in an era of man, not of gods, and he believed that we need an image of man in which to locate belief. But until *The Rock,* Stevens refused to accept an image of a man in the world as hero. In mixing the proportions between reality and the imagination, Stevens continually erred on the side of the imagination. Over and over he repeated the mistake he had cautioned against in "Examination of the Hero in a Time of War"—that the hero "be not conceived, being real."

His images of the hero were fabrications, projections, extrapolations, abstractions beyond man, preposterous shimmers or muscular giants, bare constructions in language that we certainly (to use Stevens' terms) do not recognize, much less realize, respond to, or accept.[2] His art was conceptual; the idea, and the problem it reflected, often had more interest than the thing itself; the illustration of the definition was often less convincing than the formulation of the definition. For the irresistible transcendental pull was there. But this is not an Emersonian transcendentalism. It is the courage, hubris, and naivete of a radical humanism. As Stevens put it in "The Man with the Blue Guitar," he desired something "beyond us, yet ourselves." *Beyond.* Yet even in this poem, one of the earliest to deal with the hero, the emphasis is on reality, on the hero as a means by which to reach man, a hero who could and would have been made of man, if possible:

> I cannot bring a world quite round,
> Although I patch it as I can.
>
> I sing a hero's head, large eye
> and bearded bronze, but not a man,
>
> Although I patch him as I can
> And reach through him almost to man.

After "The Man with the Blue Guitar," however, the hero becomes even less man and more god.

Stevens revealed his "prejudices" against man in a letter about "Notes Toward a Supreme Fiction." "The trouble with humanism," he wrote in 1943, "is that man as God remains man, but there is an extension of man, the leaner being, in fiction, a possibly more than human human, a composite human."[3] This is both a nostalgic notion of humanism and a desire for something more: the postulate that "man is god" is not enough, and that itself was one of our great fictions. In his extravagant optimism and equally radical doubt, Stevens wished to be the American Mallarmé, the creator of something beyond the real. But he also wanted the hero to be part of the real, not separate and autonomous from it. He wanted the best of these two possible worlds—both reality and the imagination—and this, *we* realize, was not possible. He wanted both "an extension of reality," as he put it in a slightly earlier letter, and a fiction, not the thing itself.[4]

Thus his early images of the hero are equivalent to theoretical propositions. In "Asides on the Oboe" (the title itself suggests that the hero will be off center), he proposed the dewy "impossible possible philosophers' man" and in "Chocorua to Its Neighbor," the dreamy eminence of dark blue glass, the shadowed mountain with muscular shoulders and luminous flesh. And there is also the "large-sculptured, platonic person, free from time" in "The Pure Good of Theory," the science-fiction meta-men in "The Bouquet," and the "still angelic" giant assembled part by part on the horizon:

> Here, then, is an abstraction given head,
> A giant on the horizon, given arms,
> A massive body and long legs, stretched out,
> A definition with an illustration, not
> Too exactly labelled, a large among the smalls
> Of it, a close, parental magnitude,
> At the center on the horizon, concentrum, grave
> And prodigious person, patron of origins.
>
> "A Primitive Like an Orb"

Stevens was as fancifully lavish in his period of the imagination as he was in the *Harmonium* period of reality, as we have come to call it. All these figures of the hero are constructions of the *act* of the mind, the *will* of the imagination, the *determination* of theory. None of them yielded the satisfactions of belief; they only testified to the desire of the mind for what was missing, absent.

Stevens was aware of this, of course. In more than one poem he acknowledges that these conceptions of the hero—these heroic conceptions—are ephemeral and unstable. In "A Thought Revolved," for example, the poet's search for the leader who will reconcile all opposites is qualified by an overly determined rhetorical and romantic catalogue of attributes:

> The pine, the pillar and the priest,
> The voice, the book, the hidden well,
> The faster's feast and heavy-fruited star,
> The father, the beater of the rigid drums,
>
> He that at midnight touches the guitar,
> The solitude, the barrier, the Pole
> In Paris, celui qui chante et pleure,
> Winter devising summer in its breast,
>
> Summer assaulted, thundering, illumed,
> Shelter yet thrower of the summer spear
> With all his attributes no god but man
> Of men whose heaven is in themselves.

We know that it will not work: to devise summer in the midst of winter is a contrivance of the mind, the inbred turning of thought. As Stevens further implies in the poem, this language is the product of wish-fulfillment, longed for by the poet, just as the braceleted, expiring lady of the poem's first section yearns to float off to death on the tranquilizers of Christianity.

In a much misunderstood poem which appears at the end of *Parts of a World* (1942), "Examination of the Hero in a Time of War," Stevens also calls into doubt the two major ideas (are they figures really?) of the hero which he presents: the barbarous hero, like Xenophon, who captures the unthinking allegiance of the wartime masses, and the meditative hero who abstracts himself from war. "Examination of the Hero" (the word "examination" implies a clinical inspection of appropriate qualifications, a rigorous investigation into the symptoms of the hero, who, we read again, we are to "Devise, devise") is best understood when read with "The Noble Rider and the Sound of Words," an essay also published in 1942. In both pieces, Stevens asserts that nobility is a feeling, a force, and cannot be grasped in terms of an image or person (how far we are from Eliot's notion of an objective correlative). By this, however, Stevens does not mean that there cannot be an appropriate embodiment of nobility; he understands intellectual history well enough to know that every age has its heroes and that they are real heroes for their time only. But given the unthinkable brutality of the Second World War, Stevens feared it was impossible for a man, a hero, to be adequate to his time. As described in the essay, the hero would be potent and vital, possess authority, and represent an equilibrium between the imagination and reality (we are not surprised to learn that at this point in his life, the equilibrium favored the imagination).

If Stevens could do no more than list qualities in "The Noble Rider," in "Examination of the Hero" he scrutinizes the masses cheering worn-out images of nobility, worshipping the power, not the authority, of a brutish emblem of the "hero," which is larger than human but less than civilized:

> If the hero is not a person, the emblem
> Of him, even if Xenophon, seems
> To stand taller than a person stands, has
> A wider brow, large and less human
> Eyes and bruted ears: the man-like body
> Of a primitive.

From this profanity, which turns into a macabre frivolity ("the tigers / In trombones roaring for the children"), the uncommon man, the scholar and poet, withdraws, preserving his freedom by abstracting himself from the unreal world of war heroes into a mental space where, as Stevens puts it in "A Thought Revolved," he can walk freely and sing the *idea* of the highest man. To use the terms in "The Noble Rider and the Sound of Words," the uncommon man resists the pressure of reality with an equal and opposite force of the imagination.

Although this idea is a monumental and noble one, the meditative hero limned in the poem is indulgent. In sections XIV and XV of

"Examination," Stevens heralds this hero and, just as in "A Thought Revolved," subverts his credibility through outrageous rhetoric, the glamorous flourishes which precede him:

> A thousand crystals' chiming voices,
> Like the shiddow-shaddow of lights revolving
> To momentary ones, are blended,
> In hymns, through iridescent changes,
> Of the apprehending of the hero.

And in the next section, we learn that so overwhelming is the meditative bliss of the poet (and his pastime is a mere domestic one—to study "the paper / On the wall, the lemons on the table") that the "highest man" ("self of the hero, the solar single, / Man-sun, man-moon, man-earth, man-ocean"—this is too much) emerges from it strong enough to devise the "man-man." A presumptuous result, too quickly achieved. Like Xenophon, this hero does not command our respect. In the midst of war, his meditations on wallpaper or the "syllable *fa*" seem frivolous also. His withdrawal, his abstraction, his preoccupation with "the petty gildings on February" seem inexcusable distractions, which have taken him too far from the reality of war.

Stevens is right to say earlier in the poem:

> The hero is a feeling, a man seen
> As if the eye was an emotion,
> As if in seeing we saw our feeling
> In the object seen and saved that mystic
> Against the sight, the penetrating,
> Pure eye. Instead of allegory,
> We have and are the man, capable
> Of his brave quickenings, the human
> Accelerations that seem inhuman.

Neither Xenophon nor the solipsistic poet (who has "nothing higher / Than himself, his self . . .") are capable of quickening us to bravery. The figures collapse to allegories. The meditation fades. In the last section of the poem, Stevens calls in the seasons and nostalgia, the reality principle on the one hand and the "truth" of the past on the other:

> Each false thing ends. The bouquet of summer
> Turns blue and on its empty table
> It is stale and the water is discolored.
> True autumn stands then in the doorway.
> After the hero, the familiar
> Man makes the hero artificial.
> But was the summer false? The hero?

The dazzling hero did exist, Stevens insists, but only for a moment. But is the appearance of the hero like the moment "of flickering mobility," which astute critics of Stevens read as the way he reconciles the imagination and reality, thereby creating a poetry of being?[5] I do not think so. First, it is not the reality of experience which is questioned (that is given), but the possibility of belief. Belief entails continuity, and Stevens' belief is not sustained and neither is ours. For even if we assume that the meditative hero of "Examination," the blue Chocorua, or the horizontal giant work for a moment—as long as their language lives while we read their poems—they do not give us what Stevens required of poetry in an age of disbelief: the "satisfactions of belief."[6]

I would argue further that these heroic images of the hero do not in fact work, even for a moment; they are theoretical constructions, not moments of perception. No, the summer was not false, but the analogy between the eternal return of the seasons and the life of the hero *is* false. Stevens' questions are both plaintive and shrill: "But was the summer false? The hero?" We have not yet encountered in the poem the dazzling hero of whom he speaks, and the poem's last lines, which aim to conflate the hero with summer, are overdressed, in bad taste:

> Summer, jangling the savagest diamonds and
> Dressed in its azure-doubled crimsons,
> May truly bear its heroic fortunes
> For the large, the solitary figure.

Why do these fabrications of the hero not work? Because, ironically, Stevens believed too much in the radical ability of man's imagination to create full-blown a set of myths by which to live. Stevens understood that the hero had to be transparent (we find this image throughout his work), but he did not grasp the real reasons why. For him the hero had to be beyond reality, more than man, and yet reflect reality, act as a glass through which reality could be more clearly and accurately seen.

An age does not perceive its own myths as "myth," as beyond reality, but as a part of reality; they are perceived not as fiction but as actuality. As Eliot put it, "Understanding involves an area more extensive than that of which one can be conscious; one cannot be outside and inside at the same time."[7] The Greek gods were not painted fragments of the imagination or mere mythology to the Greeks, but part of the living structure of their world. In every age there is a fiction which fits, a fiction which we believe not *as* fiction but as truth. Thus Stevens was asking the impossible when he required that we consent to his fictions of the hero as both fiction and reality. Here I am not suggesting that we should not act with courage of mind, as if something were possible when we know full well it is not. But Stevens' images of the hero do not allow us to suspend even a fraction of that disbelief. Until *The Rock*, his poetry of the hero fails, although his poetics do not. But it is not only a question of poetic failure. It is also a symptom of the twentieth-century obsession with, and over-evaluation of, doubt. What Stevens did not understand is that to succeed the hero had to be transparent not because the idea of him is abstract or because he reflects reality, but because he must be indistinguishable from reality, part of it. This demands a passion, perhaps a blind passion, which Stevens did not possess.

Myths think themselves out through men and without men's knowledge, although we strive to see our historical position as clearly as we can. And similarly, the ultimate realization of the Stevens hero thought itself out through Stevens' poems without his conscious knowledge.

Michel Benamou has read the body of Stevens' work in terms of the Jungian model of individuation, arguing that the world of reality in *Harmonium* corresponds to the personality's domination by the forces of the unconscious (the feminine principle, the earth), that the world of imagination in *Parts of a World* corresponds to the personality's domination by the forces of the conscious (the masculine hero, the intellect, the virile hero), and, finally, that the union of the two in later poems corresponds to the mature self.[8] This third stage is characterized neither by a lavish attachment to the world of reality, nor by the ascetic, heroic, masculine act of the mind, but instead by a mode of being that tempers the two impulses, which, I would argue, are only facets of the same inclination: a tenacity of mind. I agree with Helen Vendler's suggestion that in his earlier poems, Stevens seems to have "felt obliged to pretend an instinct for the fertility of the earth, when his instinct was for its austerities and dilapidations."[9] In *Harmonium* Stevens seems to will himself to embrace the "green vine angering for life," to resolve against his nature to lead a nomadic life. The poems of *Harmonium* do not so much represent the forces of the unconscious as they do Stevens' intense discipline; they are another form of the rigorous act of the mind.

Toward the end of his life and in his later poems, the "normality of the normal" and "pure being" replace, displace, the act of the mind. The pure good of theory is challenged. As Stevens explained in a letter in early 1953:

> I wanted to stay in bed and make for myself a week-end world far more extraordinary than the one that most people make for themselves. But the habitual, customary, has become, at my age, such a pleasure in itself that it is coming to be that that pleasure is at least as great as any. It is a large part of the normality of the normal. And, I suppose, that projecting this idea to its ultimate extension, the time will arrive when just to *be* will take in everything without the least *doing* since even the least doing is irrelevant to pure being.[10]

Just to *be* will yield everything, "take in everything"; "doing is irrelevant." By 1954 the Stevens hero is older and wiser. He no longer takes up arms against reality and no longer is figured as beyond reality.

This hero is foreshadowed in "The House Was Quiet and the World Was Calm," in which the mind and the text of the world become one:

> The quiet was part of the meaning, part of the mind:
> The access of perfection to the page.
>
> And the world was calm. The truth in a calm world,
> In which there is no other meaning, itself
>
> Is calm, itself is summer and night, itself
> Is the reader leaning late and reading there.

But the text still mediates the world. In "Credences of Summer,"[11] however, the "old man" stands at the center (which is not *the* center, but a center which has been posited in the mind's eye) and sees not ideas about the thing, but the thing itself. Or more accurately, the old man is the thing itself:

> It is the old man standing on the tower,
> Who reads no book. His ruddy ancientness
> Absorbs the ruddy summer and is appeased,
> By an understanding that fulfills his age,
> By a feeling capable of nothing more.

The text is no longer necessary. He reads no book. Interpretation and mediation are irrelevant to pure being. His nature ("his ruddy ancientness") corresponds to the nature of the world ("the ruddy summer"), or at least one of the seasons. Satisfactions are complete: his age is fulfilled. The old man is an eloquent image of man made in the image of Stevens himself; we respond to it deeply, as we never could to the meta-men or the abstruse impossible possible philosophers' man (here the language of contradiction stops us, we must consider the image as if it were an idea, logically). In *The Rock* the Stevens hero is part of reality and its rhythms. A wise old man, the hero of American Modernism, he is no longer a representation of something else, the imperfect exemplar of an abstraction. Nor does he live, as does the old man in "Credences of Summer," in a warm world, in "green's green apogee." In "Credences of Summer," the image of the old man is "fixed" by an act of the mind:

> Fix it in an eternal foliage
>
> And fill the foliage with arrested peace,
> Joy of such permanence, right ignorance
> Of such change possible.

In *The Rock,* the old man builds his city in snow.

II. ARGUMENTS AGAINST DEATH: "SUNDAY MORNING" AND "THE OWL IN THE SARCOPHAGUS"

In a world without heaven to follow, the stops
Would be endings, more poignant than partings, profounder,

> And that would be saying farewell, repeating farewell,
> Just to be there and just to behold.
>
> "Waving Adieu, Adieu, Adieu"

Stevens had always struggled "to suppress the merely personal."[12] To use Gertrude Stein's distinction, he struggled to speak the voice of the Human Mind, not Human Nature. That would be a voice articulated in the act of writing, not talking, a voice capable of objectivity, of living in the present and seeing things as entities, not identities, of leaving events and memories and such emotions as fear and disappointment behind, of being concerned with the weather, not personalities, of accepting death, the death of an age, the death of others, the death of the self. "Human nature," explains Stein, "can not say yes, how can human nature say yes, human nature does what it does but it cannot say yes."[13] But the Human Mind can, it can say yes.

But saying yes was for Stevens no easy achievement. If the death of the gods (and with them they took belief) was for him the cultural crisis of his age, it was also a profoundly personal problem: in it, he felt keenly the shadow of his own mortality.[14] Stevens had always known that death could not be ignored or obliterated and that we cannot take refuge in memory.[15] But it is not until *The Rock* that he confronts the fact that his own memories are an illusion, for they are no longer a part of a felt reality. Gertrude Stein put this realization in the following brisk way: "What is the use of being a little boy if you are to grow up to be a man."[16] And in his thoughtful slower way, Stevens opens "The Rock" with:

> It is an illusion that we were ever alive,
> Lived in the houses of mothers, arranged ourselves
> By our own motions in a freedom of air.

The World, as he writes in "St. Armorer's Church from the Outside," is "always beginning, over and over." Thus the continuity of the self was perhaps itself a myth, the last one that Stevens discarded. With it he discarded his former selves, but not his nature, and in their place he found satisfactions of being. As Harold Bloom has pointed out, by the end of "The Rock" "the self cites its own tranquility as means of proof, at the rock, where by opposition the mind [I would say the self] and the external realm are brought together."[17]

Death preoccupied Stevens his entire poetic life. As early as the gaudy *Harmonium* we find Stevens writing about the death of the body and sex (of course he had never really believed in the body) in the most graphic of terms:

> Our bloom is gone. We are the fruit thereof.
> Two golden gourds distended on our vines,
> Into the autumn weather, splashed with frost,
> Distorted by hale fatness, turned grotesque.

These lines are from "Le Monocle de Mon Oncle," written when he was thirty-nine and published as the eleventh poem in his *Collected Poems,* and Stevens never got any younger. But it not so much the death of the body as the death of the mind that he feared. Time is the inescapable enemy, not just because death is irrevocable, but because insistent reminders of it are everywhere—in the familiar sounds of evening, in one's heartbeat, in the rapid walk of a person going down the street:

> It is time that beats in the breast and it is time
> That batters against the mind, silent and proud,
> The mind that knows it is destroyed by time.
> > "The Pure Good of Theory"

How did a man so obsessed with death face it in his seventies and write the poems of *The Rock?* If we can answer this question, we may also better understand how Stevens reached (or discovered) the balance between the imagination and reality which he had called for in "The Noble Rider and the Sound of Words."

To see just how far Stevens has come in *The Rock,* and particularly in "To an Old Philosopher in Rome," I begin by taking a rather lengthy detour through two of his earlier poems which deal with death: first, "Sunday Morning," which I call the argument for reality, and secondly, "The Owl in the Sarcophagus," the argument for the imagination. Both arguments fail.

Although "Sunday Morning" is not in the familiar meditative mode of Stevens' poetry, its form and purpose are similar; it is a drama, to adopt Louis Martz's excellent definition, between a projected part of the self and the whole self (or mind, whose aim is to find what will suffice.)[18] Basically "Sunday Morning" is a dialogue between a brooding woman (a Jamesian character enfolded in the indolent luxuries of fine lingerie and a lazy morning) and the more articulate mind which suggests answers to her objections and questions. The poem is well known and has been much and ably discussed, so I will only summarize here. The situation is this: her agreeable musings in the midst of "bounty" are interrupted by thoughts of sacrifice and death, an expected text of a traditional American Sunday morning. And the problem is this: where on earth will she find "Things to be cherished like the thought of heaven."

Three attempts are made to answer this question. First, in section IV, it is argued that the natural world is in fact more permanent than the world of religious imagination. The cyclical view of natural history is contrasted with the Christian linear view of religious history. Her memories and anticipation of the seasons, the myth of the eternal return, the myth of continuity through change—these are stronger and more durable, it is argued, than any vague promises of a final heaven:

> There is not any haunt of prophecy,
> Nor any chimera of the grave,
> Neither the golden underground, nor isle
> Melodious, where spirits gat them home,
> Nor visionary south, nor cloudy palm
> Remote on heaven's hill, that has endured
> As April's green endures; or will endure
> Like her remembrance of awakened birds,
> Of her desire for June and evening, tipped
> By the consummation of the swallow's wings.

But she objects that the contentment nature provides her is not enough. She wants more, desiring not relative permanence but permanence absolute—"some imperishable bliss." And so in sections V and VI another argument is advanced, a more subtle and sophisticated variation of the first.

Death is personified as female, as mother. Stevens' text is that Death taketh away but first, she giveth; Death is "the mother of beauty," beauty the source of all fulfillment, indeed consummation. This strained conclusion is reached by identifying death with change, an awkward equation which results in the awkward line: "Is there no change of death in paradise?" The logical result of this identity is not only that death emerges as the Prime Mover, but heaven is rendered static and motionless, as the tomb containing the urn whose lovers never kiss. The conclusion is that our mortal earth is the true paradise.

This reasoning also is not persuasive. The woman, presumably, is beautiful and alone. Lovers who never embrace are not satisfactory. Thus Stevens turns to another argument, escalating the tone. A shrill, sexy vision of wild young men, chanting their worship of mortality, is offered:

> Supple and turbulent, a ring of men
> shall chant in orgy on a summer morn
> their boisterous devotion to the sun,
> Not as a god, but as a god might be
> Naked among them, like a savage source.

This religious rite of "heavenly fellowship," it is implied, is possible if the mortal world is acceptable as paradise—an argument which certainly seems calculated to stir at least the interest, if not the desire, of this languid woman. In fact all three arguments seem pointedly aimed at quelling her complaining and querulous tone. But none of them works. At each stage the level of rhetoric has to be heightened, increased from sweet persuasions to romantic sophistry and finally to wild imaginings.

But in the last section of the poem Stevens returns us to quieter language, acknowledging that we live not in paradise but in "island solitude, unsponsored, free / Of that wide water, inescapable." Man is alone, and the haunting idea of death returns, echoing the poem's first section. In "Sunday Morning" Stevens does not so much confront death as he illustrates an unsuccessful attempt to *reason* it away (or evaporate it by metaphor) by concentrating on the essence of *life* and *living*—change. The panacea "Death is the mother of beauty" creates an illusion for only a moment. In fact there are, we see, not two voices in the poem but three: that of the discontented woman, the devil's advocate for reality, and the more mature, resigned mind who speaks the poem's last section with tones invoking a lost American landscape:

> Deer walk upon our mountains, and the quail
> Whistle about us their spontaneous cries;
> Sweet berries ripen in the wilderness;
> And, in the isolation of the sky,
> At evening, casual flocks of pigeons make
> Ambiguous undulations as they sink,
> Downward to darkness, on extended wings.

For a moment the urban (or suburban) Sunday morning is displaced by the broad evening spaces of the American frontier, which, in reality, had closed years before. But given the argumentative structure of the poem, it is clear that this ending is not a resolution but a further appeal on the basis of the comforting, seductive mood of elegy.

If "Sunday Morning" presents the argument for reality, "The Owl in the Sarcophagus," a much later poem collected in *The Auroras of Autumn* (1950), presents the argument for the imagination. Written following the death of one of his closest friends, it is unlike any other Stevens poem. In no other piece does Stevens explore the domain of allegory, unfortunately perhaps, because this long poem is splendid. Above all a man of affirmation (Stevens once said that he stopped reading Shaw because "he had nothing affirmative in him and, also, because his noes were indiscriminate"[19]), Stevens offers a consoling, elegant dream, a sleepy and sublime "mythology of modern death," no Bosch-like visions, no Dantean hell, no grim reaper, in short, no suffering. The allegorical figures are a mirror of Stevens' will:

> The children of a desire that is the will,
> Even of death, the beings of the mind
> In the light-bound space of the mind, the floreate flare.

Not a poem which hymns the idea of the hero, "The Owl" presents what the hero might imagine, and thus is rare in the Stevens canon.

Stevens sets up the allegory within familiar conventions. A man visits the land of the dead and there meets the forms of his own thought and "dark desire." These "beings of the mind" resemble, of course, the forms of reality; the difference between them is musical and releases melancholy reverberations of remembrance and return to the Other:

And, if of substance, a likeness of the earth,
That by resemblance twanged him through and through,

Releasing an abysmal melody,
A meeting, an emerging in the light,
A dazzle of remembrance and of sight.

High sleep is a giant, characterized by the luminous revolvings of the earth, the hypnosis of a "fulfilling air," the involutions of meaning, the white of sheets, and the "ultimate intellect." Less expected and more opaque is the description of his brother Peace, who proclaims a state of peace, his authority shining in the sparkling accretions of his robes adorned with ancient, indecipherable texts:

Its brightness burned the way good solace seethes.

This was peace after death, the brother of sleep,
The inhuman brother so much like, so near,
Yet vested in a foreign absolute,

Adorned with cryptic stones and sliding shines,
An immaculate personage in nothingness,
With the whole spirit sparkling in its cloth,

Generations of the imagination piled
In the manner of its stitchings, of its thread,
In the weaving round the wonder of its need,

And by the first flowers upon it, an alphabet
By which to spell out holy doom and end,
A bee for the remembering of happiness.

Yet is the third figure who speaks most deeply to Stevens: "she that says good-by losing in self / The sense of self." Strong, desirable, and graceful, speaking not with language but the slight "backward gestures of her hand," she is not an allegorical figure (she has no name) but a "self" who has passed beyond self-consciousness. Possessing sure and inner knowledge, she speaks for those who "cannot say good-by themselves." Unlike her two brothers who represent life after death, she incarnates the moment on the edge of death, the passage between life and death. She exists in the syllable (there is no grammar here, no language that can represent this) separating the two domains:

> She was a self that knew, an inner thing,
> Subtler than look's declaiming, although she moved
> With sad splendor, beyond artifice,
> Impassioned by the knowledge that she had,
> There on the edge of oblivion.

But just as the last section of "Sunday Morning" calls into question all that went before, so the last three lines of "The Owl" confess the limits of the imagination. The regal rhetoric of thought, the sublime but much-too-comforting mythology, yield to a simpler tone. The mind which invented these figures harbors a childlike desire for the "pure perfections of parental space":

> It is a child that sings itself to sleep,
> The mind, among the creatures that it makes,
> The people, those by which it lives and dies.

The story is a bedtime tale, a fantasy which has no real authority. The myth is a fiction which is not subject to final belief. The allegory falls under the pressure of time.[20]

Stevens had warned against the problems of allegory in "Effects of Analogy." In that essay, what troubles him about Bunyan's *Pilgrim's Progress* is exactly what troubles us in "The Owl in the Sarcophagus." As we read Bunyan's story, Stevens maintains, "we are distracted by the double sense of the analogy and we are rather less engaged by the symbols than we are by what is symbolized."[21] And as we read the Stevens poem we are only too aware that it is just what the final stanza announces it is—a self-conscious mythology. The imagination, to use Stevens' own measure, does not adhere to reality. And if we take a look at the structure of the poem, we see that as an act of the mind as Stevens would define it, it falls flat. For Stevens bases his notion of the act of the mind on the principle of the *transformation* of reality. But in this poem, although each of the three figures is in itself a splendid example of the power of the imagination, the organization as a whole is so bald as to preclude the desired effect of analogy; in the words of "Effects of Analogy," the parts "do not combine, inter-act, so that one influences the other and produces an effect similar in kind to the prismatic formations that occur about us in nature in the case of reflections and refractions."[22]

The poem is organized in orderly outline fashion. It is, to transpose a phrase from a Stevens poem, merely posed.[23] In section I Stevens introduces his three allegorical characters; in section II he introduces his human character; in sections III–V he tidily describes each allegorical figure in turn; and in section VI he offers a summary and conclusion. Imagination, in other words, collapses in this poem to framework fantasy. This is not the successful, transformative act of the mind we find in such short poems as "On the Road Home" and "The Candle a Saint" or in a larger open-ended poem such as "The Man with the Blue Guitar." The argument for the imagination, we find, is no more successful in dealing with the problem of death than is the argument for reality in "Sunday Morning."

III. IT MUST BE HUMAN

Perhaps there are times of inherent excellence,

As when the cock crows on the left and all
Is well, incalculable balances,
At which a kind of Swiss perfection comes

And a familiar music of the machine
Sets up its Schwärmerei, not balances
That we achieve but balances that happen,

As a man and woman meet and love forthwith.
Perhaps there are moments of awakening,
Extreme, fortuitous, personal, in which

We more than awaken, sit on the edge of sleep,
As on an elevation, and behold
The academies like structures in a mist.

                    "Notes Toward a Supreme Fiction"

In 1954, the year of the publication of his *Collected Poems,* Stevens wrote that he had "thought of adding other sections to the NOTES and one in particular: *It Must Be Human.* "[24] *The Rock* might be called that section, for, as many have pointed out, it is the most personal and perfect group of poems which Stevens ever wrote. Poems of a wise old man, they have, as Harold Bloom has written, "an uncanny intensity and originality that surpass nearly all his previous work at middle length or shorter."[25] As Joseph Riddel has said, they are "sharply etched in Stevens' personal style, stoic and tough in the face of age's pressing questions, yet tender and knowing."[26] Stevens wrote in "Man and Winter," an earlier poem, that the "mind is the great poem of winter." In *The Rock* it is rather the poem which is the great mind of winter. Best illustrated by the perfections of "To an Old Philosopher in Rome," this meditative mind unites the self with the world. In Santayana, sheltered in the Roman convent of the Blue Nuns, we have a man, not a phantasm, as hero. In this poem, there are no questions asked, as there were in "Sunday Morning." There are no stunning acts of the imagination, as in "The Owl in the Sarcophagus." Nor is there a last-minute stanza which qualifies the hypothesis of the poem. The tone is consistently that of serene calm, deep assurance, an eloquent poise.

What is the meditative mode for Stevens? The act of the mind? The act of the imagination? Speaking generally, it would seem reasonable to call all of Stevens' poems meditative, for it was Stevens' temperament to revolve an idea in his mind, to pursue it, muse on it. But Martz cautions, and rightfully so, that we must distinguish between *imagination* and *meditation*. "Meditation," he says, "is the essential exercise which, constantly practiced, brings the imagination into play." As I pointed out earlier, Martz defines meditation as "a deliberate act of choice," "a calculated effort of the mind," "a constructive power of deliberate choice," " 'an attentive thought repeated or voluntarily maintained in the mind, to arouse the will to holy and wholesome affections and resolutions.' " It is, he says, best represented by "tightly argued, tightly ordered meditations on a theme."[27]

If we reverse (altering slightly) Martz's distinctions between meditation and imagination, defining the imagination as the heroic act of will and meditation as a state of mind, an ease of mind, an *easing* of mind, a mode of being which is sought after for its own sake, we can more clearly grasp the meditative mode of the last poems. As we recall, in "Examination of the Hero in a Time of War" Stevens describes the "highest self" this way:

> These are the works and pastimes
> Of the highest self: he studies the paper
> On the wall, the lemons on the table.

> This is his day. With nothing lost,
> He arrives at the man-man as he wanted.
> This is his night and meditation.

At that point in his life, the meditative mode was inappropriate and in-
adequate, but in his seventies this grace of mind is the result and gift of
a long life of the mind. "Sunday Morning" and "The Owl in the
Sarcophagus" are self-conscious feints against death. "To an Old
Philosopher in Rome," on the other hand, portrays Santayana, one of
the great general thinkers, near death. Santayana is one of the whole
men: "To be ruled by thought, in reality to govern ourselves by the
truth or to be able to feel that we were being governed by the truth,"
writes Stevens in his late essay "The Whole Man: Perspectives, Hori-
zons," "would be a great satisfaction. . . ."[28]

While Stevens was a student at Harvard, he met Santayana, but
although he knew the philosopher personally, their relationship was
never intimate. Stevens deeply admired Santayana as a man "of
dynamic mind . . . and something of a scholar and very much of an
original force."[29] Stevens was probably attracted to him because the
quality of their thinking was so similar: Santayana was a mirror for
Stevens. Their minds both radiate more light than heat, tend toward
balance rather than passion, and affirm the virtue of detachment rather
than testify to the tragic. Santayana's idiosyncratic combination of
naturalism and platonism finds its analogues in Stevens' notions of
reality and the imagination. Both believed, in the words of Santayana,
that poetry "adds a pure value to existence, the value of a liberal
imaginative exercise."[30] And both insisted that the world will be saved
by those who believe that the real and the ideal, reality and the imagination, must be kept in vital and dynamic interconnection.

Santayana, feeling that people and possessions were likely to be
distractions, living out the last eleven years of his life in a convent cell
with only a bed and books, must have seemed to Stevens an ideal alter
ego. In his essay "Imagination as Value," Stevens writes that Santayana is one of the few men in whose lives "the function of the
imagination has had a function similar to its function in any deliberate
work of art";[31] that function is aesthetic.

"To an Old Philosopher in Rome" opens with a metaphor of transformation which informs the entire poem. The beginning prepositional phrase is characteristically problematical:

> On the threshold of heaven, the figures in the street
> Become the figures of heaven, the majestic movement
> Of men growing small in the distances of space,
> Singing, with smaller and still smaller sound,
> Unintelligible absolution and an end—

"On the threshold of heaven" modifies two different nouns—the "Old Philosopher" of the poem's title and the "figures in the street" of the first line.[32] Both perspectives are possible and taken together constitute a paradigm of the mode of being portrayed in the poem. By both participating in and yet remaining detached from experience, Santayana becomes a figure of heaven. He could be said to transcend himself, or in the words of "The Owl in the Sarcophagus," to lose "in self / The sense of self." Here the most complete knowledge is possible: the "Extremes of the known in the presence of the extreme / Of the unknown."

The transformation of reality into something sweeter and more real occurs "easily," effortlessly. In the contact-boundary situation of death the simplest experiences of the senses are intensified and charged with aesthetic values. Harsh mutterings become "murmuring," the antiseptic smell of medicine, a fragrance. The concrete is invested with the spiritual, reality undergoes transubstantiation, and we pass from the real to the visionary with no sense of change. On the chair is a "portent," the nuns are a "moving transparence." Santayana sees the way Stevens imagined that the meta-men could see:

> The infinite of the actual perceived
> A freedom revealed, a realization touched,
> The real made more acute by an unreal.

This transformation is possible not solely by virtue of being at the edge of death, "in snow." Dignity is also required. The extreme of the unknown must be approached with control, with the self composed, with a composition of the self. And if so, Stevens suggests, more than a transformation of the real into the imagined is possible. The two worlds—the real world and its heightened, imagined counterpart, a fiction—fuse:

> The threshold, Rome, and that more merciful Rome
> Beyond, the two alike in the make of the mind.
> It is as if in a human dignity
> Two parallels become one, a perspective, of which
> Men are part both in the inch and in the mile.

Just as two parallel lines can never meet in uncurved space, so these two Romes could never have met in an ordinary situation. But here they fuse, creating a perspective from which Santayana can both see and be seen. This is the same point we discover in another poem in *The Rock,* "The Poem That Took the Place of a Mountain," the threshold from which one

> Would discover, at last, the view toward which they had edged,

> Where he could lie and, gazing down at the sea,
> Recognize his unique and solitary home.

That home is the earth, the rock, the normality of the normal.

In the process of discovering that perspective toward which one had moved cautiously, perhaps throughout a lifetime, the figure of the self, "losing in self / The sense of self," paradoxically grows more distinct. The poem's structure parallels this process, progressively focusing our attention on the figure of Santayana. The poem has three parts: in the first (stanzas 1–6), Santayana does not appear; in the second (stanzas 7–11), Stevens points him out; and in the third (stanzas 12–16), Santayana dominates the field. The final lesson of the master is the belief that the whole of life can be the formation of a gestalt in time, the coherent course of a particular. As Santayana wrote in his preface to *Realms of Being,* "Our distinction and glory, as well as our sorrow, will have lain in being something in particular, and in knowing what that is."[33]

In the second section of the poem Stevens asks Santayana to be the man who can speak for all mankind—a moving and courageous request, for Stevens is demanding it of himself also:

> So that we feel, in this illumined large,
> The veritable small, so that each of us
> Beholds himself in you, and hears his voice
> In yours, master and commiserable man.

Years before Stevens had said bluntly that the chief defect of humanism was that it concerned human beings.[34] Now, accepting a man as both "master" and "commiserable" who in creating a "total edifice" composed a self, and who "says good-by by losing in self / The sense of self," Stevens writes that "It is poverty's speech which seeks us out most." If Pound's achievement, given his proud temperament, in the *Pisan Cantos* is humility, Stevens' achievement in *The Rock* is to move beyond the act of the mind into the integrated realm of being.

This realm of being has its own mode of meditation. Stevens describes Santayana as "half-asleep," both "dozing in the depths of wakefulness" and "intent," not "intent" in the sense of strenuous concentration but rather in the sense of absorption, fascination, interest. In "To an Old Philosopher in Rome" it is not speculation on a fiction that gives happiness and peace, but absorption in the particular, the smell of medicine, "the particles of nether-do." This is the poet's condition of "vague receptivity" which Stevens describes in his late essay "A Collect of Philosophy."[35] It is the "vivid sleep" of "The Rock," and the "ease of the mind that was like being alone in a boat at sea" in "Prologues to What Is Possible." What is possible are "not balances / That we achieve but balances that happen," as he called such moments in "Notes Toward a Supreme Fiction."

Thus these poems of *The Rock* record Stevens' movement beyond the disciplined, deliberate act of the mind into a condition of receptivity to experience. As he wrote in a letter in 1950 about the privacy which Hartford offered him: "It seems easier to think here. Perhaps this is balanced by the possibility that one has less to think about or, rather, less occasion to think. Yet that does not seem possible. Then, too, it is not always easy to tell the difference between thinking and looking out of the window."[36] This is an admission of immense proportions. This mode of being suspends doubt. Introspection and perception here merge for Stevens. The old Stevens problem of the subject-object split, the old problem of clearing away everything that comes between the perceiving mind and the world as perceived, has disappeared along with the problem of belief. In "To an Old Philosopher in Rome" the categories of subject and object cannot really be said to exist. Instead we find an easy interpenetration between the outside and the inside. The sound of the bells drifts in.

And now we understand exactly what Stevens means by the world as meditation. In the beautiful poem of that title, Penelope, waiting for Ulysses, composes a self—she does not postulate a supreme fiction—with which to meet and be in the world. With Penelope it is not an act of the mind that sustains her, but a confidence in her own strength and an acceptance of the "inhuman meditation of the world," the round of time and the seasons. She waits, patiently. Her "barbarous energy" and her receptivity to the particulars of experience—to daybreak and spring—allow her to receive the rising sun as she would Ulysses, as if it were Ulysses. As in "To an Old Philosopher in Rome" where the city of Rome and heaven become one, where the whole shape of Rome is repeated in the shape of the bed, in "The World as Meditation" her meditation parallels the "inhuman meditation." The two come together:

> The two kept beating together. It was only day.
> It was Ulysses and it was not. Yet they had met,
> Friend and dear friend and a planet's encouragement.
> The barbarous strength within her would never fail.

And with it, the "inhuman meditation" becomes "a planet's encouragement." Penelope's "barbarous strength" is not like the strength of mind which Nietzsche possessed. Of Nietzsche, Stevens had written, "In his mind one does not see the world more clearly . . . a strong mind distorts the world."[37] In their strength neither Penelope nor Santayana distort the world; they are in rhythm with it.

If in the second part of "To an Old Philosopher in Rome" Stevens asks Santayana to speak "Profound poetry of the poor and of the dead," in the third section the figure of the philosopher becomes that orator "with accurate tongue / And without eloquence":

> And you—it is you that speak it, without speech,
> The loftiest syllables among loftiest things,
> The one invulnerable man among
> Crude captains, the naked majesty, if you like,
> Of bird-nest arches and of rain-stained vaults.

It is not simple speech which Santayana offers but the very elements of language—its syllables. "We say ourselves in syllables that rise," Stevens wrote in "The Creations of Sound," "from the floor, rising in speech we do not speak." The absolution Santayana grants is "unintelligible." The message is not the text he had composed but the man himself. These are "the immaculate syllables" Stevens spoke of in "The Men That Are Falling": "That he spoke only by doing what he did."

Stevens, we remember, once said that the simplest personification of the angel of reality would be the good man. If earlier in "To an Old Philosopher in Rome" the figure of Santayana is "impatient for the grandeur" that he needs in "so much misery," now the desire to escape is replaced by a total commitment to the real: "The life of the city never lets go, nor do you / Ever want it to." Santayana is both alone and not alone. He is at one with the city just as Penelope is at one with the weather. Like the man in "An Ordinary Evening in New Haven," "Life fixed him," always watching:

> This sat beside his bed, with its guitar,
> To keep him from forgetting, without a word,
> A note or two disclosing who it was.

A temporary stay against death has been granted:

> It is a kind of total grandeur at the end,
> With every visible thing enlarged and yet
> No more than a bed, a chair and moving nuns,
> The immensest theatre, the pillared porch,
> The book and candle in your ambered room,
> Total grandeur of a total edifice,
> Chosen by an inquisitor of structures
> For himself. He stops upon his threshold,
> As if the design of all his words takes form
> And frame from thinking and is realized.

The "total edifice" which stands as shelter is the self that he has composed through the act of writing. As Stevens says of himself in "The Planet on the Table" (and it applies to Santayana):

> His self and the sun were one
> And his poems, although makings of his self,
> Were no less makings of the sun.

The flow and fear of time, the movement of the opening stanza, are stopped; Santayana lives completely within the present, "the normality of the normal." The poem's ending has the quality of apocalypse, of a monumental, visionary, and yet simple human poise. Stevens dramatizes what he had hoped for years before in "The Man with the Blue Guitar":

> A tune beyond us as we are,
> Yet nothing changed by the blue guitar;
>
> Ourselves in the tune as if in space,
> Yet nothing changed, except the place
>
> Of things as they are and only the place
> As you play them, on the blue guitar,
>
> Placed, so, beyond the compass of change,
> Perceived in a final atmosphere;
>
> For a moment final, in the way
> The thinking of art seems final when
>
> The thinking of god is smoky dew.

But there is one important difference. In this much earlier poem all Stevens could hope for was that this "tune" would last for a "moment." And as we know, much of Stevens' poetry is a poetry of evanescence and epiphany. But in "To an Old Philosopher in Rome" the still point is not a single heightened moment. It is a quiet state of being, it is a point of perspective on one's entire life. And this applies to the opening poem of *The Rock,* "An Old Man Asleep," just as it does to Stevens' final collection of poems as a whole. The mood is one of elegy and farewells in keeping with Stevens' "wintry temperament,"[38] as Helen Vendler has so aptly called it. But it is predominately that of quiet confidence, of Stevens' acceptance of what his life has been (the poems he has written—these, not memories—are the testaments to his life) and what his life could be now.

To review. In "To an Old Philosopher in Rome," we read how a man—Stevens—might live out the end of his life with nobility. The wise man, building his city in snow, must confront death rather than reason it away or lull himself to sleep with a "modern mythology." Reality must be bared to its essentials, the luxury of peignoirs and green freedom of cockatoos rejected for the poverty of "No more than a bed, a chair and moving nuns." There must be a "dignity" won through "a solitude of the self," as we read in "Things of August":

> When was it that the particles became
> The whole man, that tempers and beliefs became
> Temper and belief and that differences lost
> Difference and were one? It had to be
> In the presence of a solitude of the self,
> An expanse and the abstraction of an expanse,
> A zone of time without the ticking of clocks,
> A color that moves us with forgetfulness.
> Where was it that we heard the voice of union?

And finally, the dominating act of mind must yield to a mode of meditation, which is a mode of being, characterized by receptivity to experience.

"Poetry," says Stevens in *Adagia*, "is health." Of all his collections, *The Rock* is the only one which offers the satisfactions of health. For the problem of belief no longer concerned him with the same intensity. In his last poems we see Stevens content to meet the normal, the everyday, every day, as Penelope does in "The World as Meditation." As he said in a letter in 1949:

> ... what one ought to find is normal life, insight into the commonplace, reconciliation with every-day reality. The things that it makes me happy to do are things of this sort. . . . At the moment what I have in mind is a group of things which mean a good deal more than they sound like meaning: for instance, airing the house in the morning; the colors of sunlight on the side of the house; people in their familiar aspects. All this is difficult for me. It is possible that pages of insight and or reconciliation, etc. are merely pages of description. The trouble is that poetry is so largely a matter of transformation. To describe a cup of tea without changing it and without concerning oneself with some extreme aspect of it is not at all the easy thing that it seems to be.[39]

The Rock moves closer and closer to the bone of the ''normal life.'' Beginning with ''An Old Man Asleep'' (who not only can possess two worlds but does), moving unself-consciously to the myth before the myth began (the father, the rock at ''the spirit's base'' in ''The Irish Cliffs of Moher''), and from there to the sad emptiness of ''The Plain Sense of Things'' and ''Long and Sluggish Lines,''[40] *The Rock* ends with an unpretentious poem entitled ''Not Ideas about the Thing but the Thing Itself.'' And Stevens means it.

The old man half asleep in the winter of *The Rock* wakes up in early March to the ''scrawny cry'' of the earliest bird. Like Penelope, he believes in the ''inhuman meditation of the world,'' that the ''chorister'' would be followed by the ''choir'' of spring and that this was and would be enough. It is no longer a question of satisfying the mind. The triumph is that the cry is not ''a sound in his mind,'' not willed into being by his dreaming imagination (''the vast ventriloquism / Of sleep's faded papier-mache''), but outside. The cry is reality, a song of fixed accord which will be heard every day, and each day will be ''like / A new knowledge of reality.''

This is what he wants—a quiet normal life, as he calls it in the title of one of his last poems—for ''transcendent forms'' have no more vitality for him, ''but his actual candle blazed with artifice.'' This is what Stevens means in the long poem ''The Rock.'' The fictive covering of reality is not enough, the poem as icon is not enough:

> It is not enough to cover the rock with leaves.
> We must be cured of it by a cure of the ground
> Or a cure of ourselves, that is equal to a cure
>
> Of the ground, a cure beyond forgetfulness.
> And yet the leaves, if they broke into bud,
> If they broke into bloom, if they bore fruit,
>
> And if we ate the incipient colorings
> Of their fresh culls might be a cure of the ground.

The world, Stevens knew and had known for a long time, was made by man in the image of man. But Stevens learned that it is not enough to recognize that fact. Man must live in the world, he must love the world, he must eat its fruit: ''They bloom as a man loves, as he lives in love / They bear their fruit so that the year is known." In "The Rock" reality is linked with singleness and grayness, and the imagination is linked with the potency of the diverse. In "Note on Moonlight" Stevens reverses similar terms: the "'one moonlight" (the imagination, the sense of the poet) and "the various universe" (the rock, reality). But what is important in both these poems is not so much these distinctions between two aspects of the world, but the conclusion that the world is the source of tranquility and that the satisfactions of tranquility are at last so easily arrived at:

> The one moonlight, the various universe, intended
> So much just to be seen—a purpose, empty
> Perhaps, absurd perhaps, but at least a purpose,
> Certain and ever more fresh. Ah! Certain, for sure . . .

1. As Helen Vendler observes in *On Extended Wings: Wallace Stevens' Longer Poems* (Cambridge, Mass.: Harvard University Press, 1969), the last line of "Like Decorations in a Nigger Cemetery" is "a remark . . . not an accomplishment" (p. 67).

2. Stevens makes this distinction between "recognize" and "realize" in "The Noble Rider and the Sound of Words," *The Necessary Angel: Essays on Reality and the Imagination* (New York: Vintage, 1951); he says of Plato's figure for the soul, "We recognize it perfectly. We do not realize it. We understand the feeling of it, the robust feeling, clearly and fluently communicated. Yet we understand it rather than participate in it" (pp. 6–7).

3. Letter from Wallace Stevens to Hi Simons, January 12, 1943, in Wallace Stevens, *Letters,* ed. Holly Stevens (New York: Alfred A. Knopf, 1966), p. 434.

4. Letter from Wallace Stevens to Henry Church, December 8, 1942, in *Letters,* p. 431.

5. This is the phrase of J. Hillis Miller. See his "Wallace Stevens' Poetry of Being," in *The Act of the Mind,* eds. Roy Harvey Pearce and J. Hillis Miller (Baltimore: Johns Hopkins University Press, 1965), p. 240. See also Thomas G. Hines' *The Later Poetry of Wallace Stevens: Phenomenological Parallels with Husserl and Heidegger* (Lewisburg: Bucknell University Press, 1976), in which he argues that "the supreme fiction, for Stevens, was the Poetry of Being" (p. 141).

6. *Opus Posthumous* (New York: Alfred A. Knopf, 1966), p. 206.

7. T. S. Eliot, *Notes toward a Definition of Culture* (London: Faber and Faber, 1948), p. 41.

8. See Michel Benamou, *L'Oeuvre→Monde de Wallace Stevens* (Paris: Honoré Champion, 1975) for a discussion of the whole of Wallace Stevens using this approach.

9. Quoted in Harold Bloom, *Wallace Stevens: The Poems of Our Climate* (Ithaca: Cornell University Press, 1977), p. 76.

10. Letter from Wallace Stevens to José Rodriguez Feo, January 13, 1953, in *Letters,* p. 767.

11. The change that occurs in Stevens' poetry can be seen by comparing the apparent ease of achievement, simple language, and calm tone of this poem with the last section of "The Pure Good of Theory":

> And yet remains the same, the beast of light
> Groaning in half-exploited gutturals
>
> The need of its element, the final need
> Of final access to its element—
> Of access like the page of a wiggy book,
> Touched suddenly by the universal flare
> For a moment, a moment in which we read and repeat
> The eloquence of light's faculties.

12. Letter from Wallace Stevens to Harvey Breit, July 29, 1942, in *Letters,* p. 413.

13. Gertrude Stein, *Geographical History of America or the Relation of Human Nature to the Human Mind* (New York: Vintage, 1973), p. 133.

14. Stevens, we should remember, was never able to obtain life insurance because his blood pressure was considered too high; he was once told by a doctor that he might be dead by the age of forty.

15. Explaining a portion of "Notes Toward a Supreme Fiction," Stevens wrote to Hi Simons, January 12, 1943 (*Letters,* p. 434), "We cannot ignore or obliterate death, yet we do not live in memory. Life is always new; it is always beginning. The fiction is part of this beginning."

16. *Geographical History of America,* p. 58.

17. *Wallace Stevens: The Poems of Our Climate,* p. 357.

18. See Martz's *Poem of the Mind.*

19. Letter from Wallace Stevens to Thomas McGreevy, April 13, 1951, in *Letters,* p. 715.

20. Joseph Riddel ("Walt Whitman and Wallace Stevens: Functions of a 'Literatus,'" in *Wallace Stevens: A Collection of Critical Essays,* ed. Marie Borroff [Englewood Cliffs, N.J.: Prentice-Hall, 1963], p. 36) argues that this "mythology" is persuasive: "the consolations of a poetry which celebrates death as fundamental with life's rhythms, a final punctuation just as sleep and rest are intermediate punctuations, pauses relative to the sense of rhythm itself." But this interpretation makes no logical sense: death cannot possibly exist both within life and at the same time be a "final punctuation." But the fact that this is a logical impossibility would be irrelevant if the poem itself performed the necessary transformation to make the paradox convincing.

21. *The Necessary Angel,* p. 109.

22. *The Necessary Angel,* p. 109.

23. "Add This to Rhetoric."

24. Letter from Wallace Stevens to Robert Pack, December 28, 1954, in *Letters*, pp. 863–64.

25. *Wallace Stevens: The Poems of Our Climate*, p. 338.

26. Joseph Riddel, *The Clairvoyant Eye: The Poetry and Poetics of Wallace Stevens* (Baton Rouge: Louisiana State University Press, 1965), p. 243.

27. Various quotations from *The Poem of the Mind*.

28. *Opus Posthumous*, p. 235.

29. Letter from Wallace Stevens to Henry Church, October 15, 1950, in *Letters*, p. 378.

30. Quoted in *The Development of American Philosophy*, ed. Walter G. Muedler, Laurence Sears, and Anne V. Schaback (Cambridge: Houghton Mifflin, 1960), p. 260.

31. *The Necessary Angel*, p. 147.

32. In the first case, the dying Santayana, looking down at the people in the street from his window (the favored Stevens' position for a poet), perceives the buzz of reality as more meaningful to him than normal, larger than normal, heavenly. But it is a heaven that is receding from him, growing fainter, and finally fading. In the second case, everyone on the "threshold" of death, including Santayana, becomes greater ("figures of heaven") and thus recedes from *us;* and although their absolution (of us) remains a mystery, the example of their "majestic movement" remains. I therefore disagree with Helen Vendler, who believes that only one or the other are possible at any moment. She writes, "The venerable mind belongs to what Stevens will call the Omega in man, peering forever into distances. Credences of summer are only possible when that aspect of the mind is suspended by an effort [in the late poems, I would say that no effort is involved], so that for a moment the present can suffice and the distant can 'fail' the normally clairvoyant eye" (*On Extended Wings*, p. 243).

33. *The Development of American Philosophy*, p. 463.

34. Letter from Wallace Stevens to Henry Church, May 18, 1943, in *Letters*, p. 449.

35. *Opus Posthumous*, p. 197.

36. Letter from Wallace Stevens to Barbara Church, February 1, 1950, in *Letters*, p. 664.

37. Letter from Wallace Stevens to Henry Church, December 8, 1942, in *Letters*, p. 431.

38. *On Extended Wings*, p. 47.

39. Letter from Wallace Stevens to Barbara Church, July 27, 1949, in *Letters*, p. 643.

40. Here I must disagree with Helen Vendler in her epilogue to her excellent book *On Extended Wings*. Given the undisputed vitality of Wallace Stevens' last poems, I find her comments surprising. She speaks of his "decrepitude" (p. 308), the "looseness," "lack of forward motion," and "ruminativeness" that characterize his old age and some of his poems (p. 309), and finally, the theme

of the man become child, which appears in his late poems (''his west touches his east,'' p. 310). Although we do encounter the image of the child in Stevens' last poems, I would like to see it considered more thoroughly before it is pronounced an image of second childhood, for Vendler's notion of old age in Stevens reflects too easily the negative stereotype of old age.

5

WILLIAM CARLOS WILLIAMS AND *PATERSON V*
Tradition and the Individual Talent

By it they mean that when I have suffered . . . I too shall run for cover;
that I too shall seek refuge in fantasy. And mind you, I do not say that I
will not. To decorate my age. —I Wanted to Write a Poem[1]

In the opening of the fifth book of *Paterson* it could be Stevens speaking, it could be Eliot. This Williams must have known when he began with an unmistakable reference to the rock of Stevens, the March of Stevens, and the birds of Stevens' last piece in his *Collected Poems,* which speak not prophecy but are the thing itself. And just a few pages later in *Paterson V* we hear the voice of Eliot's *Four Quartets* intoning "What but indirection / will get to the end of the sphere?" Certainly it is surprising that Williams should take this as his text, but it is even more surprising that in the last part of *Paterson V* he should expand the text into Eliotic testimony of religious experience and triumph over time and death:

> The (self) direction has been changed
>   the serpent
>   its tail in its mouth
> "the river has returned to its beginnings"
>   and backward
>   (and forward)
> it tortures itself within me
>   until time has been washed finally under:
>   and "I knew all (or enough)
> it became me   .   "
>
>   .   .
>
>   [I, iii]

Eliot and Stevens—these are the two poets in the American Modern tradition one would least expect Williams to honor. Yet honor them he does and, in fact, he could be said to join their ranks. For in the seven years between the publication of the fourth and fifth books of *Pater-*

son, between 1951 and 1958, Williams and his poetry underwent a profound change.

In 1951 Williams suffered his first stroke and was forced to retire. Three years later he published *The Desert Music and Other Poems*, a transition volume marked on the one hand by energy, confidence, and curiosity in the "local" and on the other by an almost desperate confusion in the face of an exhausted and weak old age. Of these two extremes, marked by "The Desert Music" and "For Eleanor and Bill Monahan," "The Desert Music" came first.

"I must gather together the stray ends of what I have been thinking," Williams wrote to Louis Martz after his stroke, "and make my full statement as to their meaning or quit."[2] "The Desert Music," a long poem about his brief trip across the Mexican border in 1950, does just this. Written in the manner of the first four books of *Paterson*, it deals with essentially the same problem but accomplishes what they never could—it glorifies the city. In Mexico Williams finds the poetic line to celebrate this city of paper flowers and dried peppers, poverty and laughing young girls. Talking and walking, drinking and carrying on, here Williams is *in* the city, a real part of it, not, as he often is in the first four books of *Paterson*, a silent observer whose near-allegorical mission is literally to conceive its inhabitants. "Desert Music" is not a poem of reminiscence, of an agony of descent, or of memory, as some have read it, but a poem of action and characteristic Williams shoulder-to-shoulder contact with a living culture, the local, the real.[3]

Why was this possible in Juárez and El Paso and not in Paterson, New Jersey? All these cities are stamped by poverty. But in the south Williams discovers a culture which is full of color, music, and a people who are alive, vital, and vibrant. The reason: these people are the descendants, the survivors, of the Aztec culture which Williams rapturously idealized and which, he had more than once mused, could have been "the pure American addition to world culture."[4] Latins, Spanish Indians, Mexicans, displaced white Americans—what is most important is that these people have not divorced the soul from the body. As we see even in "Desert Music," Williams believed that it is from the association of the body and the soul—even a perverse association—that a healing and glorifying poetry of the city is born.

The scene, for example, is a tourist-trap dump of a bar. The form of beauty is "flagrant" (as it often is in *Paterson*), an un-American (yet more truly American) version of the female, lower class, with whom Williams is so obsessed in the first four books of *Paterson*. An old whore in a sequined G-string does bumps and grinds to the incongruous song of soul and love. But nonetheless, almost unaccountably, the body is linked to the soul, and from this "worn-out trouper from / the States" (from "slime") comes "so sweet a tune":[5]

Andromeda of those rocks
the virgin of her mind   .   those unearthly
greens and reds

in her mockery of virtue
she becomes unaccountably virtuous   .
though she in no
way pretends it   .

.   .   .   .

What in the form of an old whore in
a cheap Mexican joint in Juárez, her bare
can waggling crazily can be
so refreshing to me, raise to my ear
so sweet a tune, built of such slime?

This is the music of poetry, "a protecting music." "I am a poet!" Williams writes triumphantly, "*I* / am.   I am."

"The Desert Music" is Williams' strongest affirmation of both his power as a poet and the power of poetry as a "music of survival." Sadly, it is also his last muscular, masculine poem and as such would appear the appropriate sequel to *Paterson IV,* a better *Paterson V* than the poem itself. For Williams, the poem had always been the locus of the body and mind (or the imagination, as Williams often calls it), and this is achieved, with vigor, in "Desert Music." The triumph is all the more moving because Williams was struggling against physical odds; the constant fear is that the mind will be weakened also. Moreover, necessarily the relationship between the body and the mind (and it was always an intimate connection for Williams) must change, and thus we may not be surprised to see that after "Desert Music," Williams' notion of what a poem is also changes; the mind now lives first and foremost in words, not the body.

As we read in the poignant "To Daphne and Virginia,"

> Be patient that I address you in a poem,
> there is no other
> fit medium.
> The mind
> lives there. It is uncertain,
> can trick us and leave us
> agonized. But for resources
> what can equal it?
> There is nothing. We
> should be lost
> without its wings to
> fly off upon.

If Williams' notion of poetry changes with age and physical infirmity, we might also observe that so do his poetic mode and his poetic line (the physical ease of his triadic line has been explicitly linked to his difficulties in reading after his strokes by Jerome Mazzaro in his splendid study of the late poems of Williams).[6] The fertile profusion of rhythms, the open form, the voices of everyday speech of "Desert Music"—all contract to the meditative religious chant of the not-so variable foot in "For Eleanor and Bill Monahan." In this strange poem Williams confesses to an anguish, weakness, loss of potency, and confusion about his sexual identity (something, it must be said, which he had rarely if *ever* felt before or admitted). In an almost self-pitying meditative address to the Virgin Mary he declares her (in, however, true Williams irreverent fashion) both "young and fit to be loved." But the lament is that *he* is not fit to do it. Not only is he "half man and half / woman," but worse, he does not have the will:

> But I
> am an old man. I
> have had enough.

This must be understood as one of the most intimate of Williams' confessions. Pound he had charged with the sin of having developed "androgynetically from the past itself mind to mind." The sign of Pound's sin, Williams believed, was his refusal of the form of the present and his hope for a return of "political, social and economic autocracy."[7] This is, we could infer, what Williams feared for himself and for that reason he appealed for help from the Virgin Mary:

> The female principle of the world
>   is my appeal
>   in my extremity
> to which I have come.
>   *O clemens! O pia! O dolcis!*
>   *Maria.*

In *Journey to Love,* published a scant year later, it would seem that this appeal had once and for all been answered. The extremes of mood of the previous volume have disappeared, and in their place we find a calm persistence and pervading tone of reminiscence. Overshadowed by the world of memory, the world of particulars shrinks to an occasional window sparrow, a bus station drunk, or a look in his son's eyes. But by and large, "the hollows of the eyes," as he says in "Shadows," "are unpeopled." All no longer depends on the celebrated red wheelbarrow and its white chickens for, as he puts it in the major, and by far the longest, poem of the book, "Asphodel, That Greeny Flower," which he had orginally conceived as the sequel to *Paterson IV* and later rejected:

> Approaching death,
>   as we think, the death of love,
>   no distinction
> any more suffices to differentiate
>   the particulars
>   of place and condition
> with which we have been long
>   familiar.

The outlines are blurred, he says; they cannot help him know what he must know about his own death if it is to be "real." It is, in other words, not place, not particulars, which can give him either peace or meaning. Although too simple a formulation, we might say that his creed has become in a very real sense no longer the famous tenet "no ideas but in things" but the opposite—"no things but in ideas."

In this volume of poems, as its title suggests, it is a tender love which gives his world meaning. It is love associated with light and imagination, a trinity with which the Virgin Mary of "To Eleanor and Bill Monahan" could be said to have answered him. From this trinity of love, the memory of the asphodel takes on a significance which it is too frail to bear:

> Light, the imagination
> > and love,
> > > in our age,
> by natural law,
> > which we worship
> > > maintain
> all of a piece
> > their dominance.

The rhythms of "Asphodel" are leisurely and rambling. Here the feminine principle is no longer associated with sexual urges and strong rhythms of accumulation and release, but rather with the principle of duration, a long and lasting marriage. Significantly, in this poem the issue of sex, long a central preoccupation in Williams' work, is not even a mere question. *Journey to Love* in fact is the first—and only— book in which it does not even appear. Perhaps for Williams sex had to die before the other could fully develop—first sex, then love. We know that this is the line of succession upon which he entered his marriage. Perhaps this is what he means when he writes:

> You understand
> > I had to meet you
> > > after the event
> and still have to meet you.
> > Love
> > > to which you too shall bow
> along with me—

But this delicate balance of love, light, and the imagination with its too sweet interplay between love and the memory of the emblematic flower did not sustain Williams for long. Nor, I might add, does it hold our attention as poetry. We read it with more interest as an autobiographical piece than we do for its lyrical delicacy or psychological truth. Although as readers we want to admire what we take to be Williams' candor and wish not to be harsh with an old man's bedlocked confessions, nevertheless to be honest we must question the quality of the poem in terms of both its artistic achievement and its moral dimension, for the two are explicitly connected in the poem. Certainly the poem has moments of lyric fineness and compression, but for the most part it is strung together on the loose and unconvincing principle of the *Autobiography:* one incident yields to another; Williams writes to keep on writing. Just as we do not learn in his *Autobiography* what the "hidden core" of his life is (and we suspect that perhaps he did not know either), in "Asphodel" we do not see how his absolution is won. He opens the poem asking for forgiveness from his wife (the symbol of their love, the asphodel, he writes in a touching phrase, has a "moral order"); he presents himself alternately as anguished and self-vaunting, and he closes the poem asserting that she has indeed forgiven him:

> You have forgiven me
> > making me new again.

We want to agree, with some relief, but it is difficult to see the poetic means by which this forgiveness is gotten. I do not wish to beat an old man's poem to death, but "Asphodel" raises a serious poetic problem. The long poem was not Williams' strength, nor was, it must be admitted, prose. To achieve a basic transformation of feeling is perhaps a dramatic art which he did not possess. This point I will come back to later.

Nothing if not a consistently restless and courageous man, who perhaps overextended himself, Williams could not rest with the unchallenging sweetness of "Asphodel." In 1958 *Paterson V* was published. Acclaimed a masterpiece—and that it surely is—*Book V* does, as few tire of pointing out, affirm-the-triumph-of-the-imagination-over-death-and-old-age. But, *Paterson V*, as this paean might lead one to expect, is not just a variation on the theme of "Asphodel." This is his most complex meditative poem, and as a poem "du Vieux Sage" it differs radically from all others he had written. How does *V* depart from the first four books of *Paterson?* Does *V* fulfill or disappoint our expectations of Williams? How can we understand the change which occurred between the first four books and the fifth? And how does the kind of peace which Williams makes for himself compare with what Pound finds in the *Pisan Cantos*, Eliot finds in the *Four Quartets*, and Stevens finds in *The Rock?* These are questions that are considered in this chapter.

I. TENOCHTITLAN AS THE AMERICAN UTOPIA

> One is at liberty to guess what the pure American addition to world culture might have been if it had gone forward singly. But that is merely an academicism. Perhaps Tenochtitlan which Cortez destroyed held the key. That also is beside the point, except that Tenochtitlan with its curious brilliance may still legitimately be kept alive in thought not as something which *could* have been preserved but as something which was actual and was destroyed.—''The American Background''[8]

A self-appointed creator of American culture, Williams understood his mission when he conceived *Paterson* in its four books as that of making the American city real, of bringing into being an articulate whole. As he put it in the preface:

> To make a start
> out of particulars
> and make them general, rolling
> up the sum. . . .

By 1958 however, he had shifted from the provincial in the American grain to the Western universal in European art. If before his object was to make the American city real, in *Book V* his object is to make art real. Accordingly, in *Book V* the overlying allegorical structure— the poet as city—is flatly dropped. Williams is no longer a heavily populated Paterson wanting to give voice to his thoughts, the people. Rather he is a private person who has little to do with the noise of the city and all to do with the quiet of a museum. In *Book V* the tone is no longer predominantly that of aggressive pursuit of the city's geography, its workers, books, and Sunday afternoons. Instead it is meditative, reminiscent, and largely lyrical. The flat and jagged edge of prose has almost entirely disappeared, and with it has disappeared the concern with American history. The American Indian is replaced by the huntsman and unicorn of medieval legend. The lower class, scarred, "cheap" black woman ("Beautiful Thing") is displaced by the aristocratic maiden of the French tapestries. Tradition, in short, supersedes, or at least surrounds, individual (local) talent.

What does this radical shift of priorities mean? It means for Williams failure in the attempt to make the local universal. It means failure in the attempt to realize in the American city a sustaining culture. It means, to use one of the dominant metaphors of the first four books, divorce from the city. Moreover it means an acceptance of the long-familiar and long-rejected position of Pound and Eliot—that the tradition of other cultures can give sustenance where our own wasteland cannot. Here the objection may be raised that *Book V* is to be understood simply as Williams' metacommentary on the art of writing in reference to the first four books of *Paterson*.[9] But this hypothesis too easily avoids the troublesome problem of the subject matter and origin of the very two examples of art which he focuses on—the fifteenth-century French tapestries housed at New York City's Cloisters and Peter Breughel's Nativity. This is what Williams chose, not, as one might have expected from his American background, native American sources for his myths, or twentieth-century American painters and photographers (a Charles Sheeler or an Alfred Stieglitz, for example) for his art. In *Book V* it is as though he had never written his brilliant, precocious, and passionate book *In the American Grain*. It is as though he could no longer write a "Desert Music."

This being understood, the fruitful approach, in other words, is not to struggle with reconciling the unexpected ground of *Book V* with the rest of Williams' work, but to come to terms with the very significant differences which exist. And the suspicion inevitably occurs. Was Williams running off to the peripheries, as he had accused Pound and Eliot of doing? Would it be fair to characterize him as a "subtle conformist," as he himself had once characterized Eliot?[10] Would it be accurate to say that in *Book V* Williams chooses caviar, not bread; that he reveals a taste for the exquisite which he had more than once associated with Pound?[11] It seems fair to say he does.

The basic opposition set up in the whole of *Paterson* thus can be defined as the conflict between culture (American) and art, or alternatively put, the city and the museum. The two, it is clear, cannot be reconciled; neither can contain meaningfully or for long the other. Just why this is so has much to do with Williams' concept of the city and his notion of culture. Consider *Paterson* itself. The first four books are built on the almost mystical and twin belief that man is defined by the city which he has built and lives in, and that the city itself is a living organism defined not only by its parts (its people) but also by its relationship to its surrounding landscape as well. Like the twentieth-century visionary architect Paolo Soleri, Williams sees the city as more than a machinelike sum of its parts. There is an interpenetration between the city and water and land, an identification between city and a new kind of man. More importantly, the city is a work of art, a moral entity.

Thus Williams chooses a passage from Santayana as the epigraph to *Book III*, "The Library":

> Cities, for Oliver, were not a part of nature. He could hardly feel, he could hardly admit even when it was pointed out to him, that cities are a second body for the human mind, a second organism, more rational, permanent and decorative than the animal organism of flesh and bone: a work of natural yet moral art, where the soul sets up her trophies of action and instruments of pleasure.

A fitting introduction to *Book III*, perfect because it could not be integrated into the main text, only contrasted to it. For *Book III* turns on the contradiction between city and museum. Instead of "library" read "museum," a museum of books which the poet decimates by an all powerful blast of the imagination, which he destroys by fire, wind, and flood. "The Library is desolation, it has a smell of its own / stagnation and death": it is a prison of "Dead men's dreams" which threatens to absorb the artist, to black out his consciousness, to possess and oppress him in the past. For the books are hollow. Like the Puritans Williams describes in *In the American Grain*, they are shells only, they lack life. As he writes in familiar metaphor as late as 1954 in his preface to his *Selected Essays*, "Masterpieces are only beautiful in a tragic sense, like a starfish lying stretched dead on the beach in the sun."[12]

The reason for this, he explains in "An Approach to the Poem," is that the work of art lives only in the period in which it is created. It has a finite historical life. The "monumental poems of the past," he says, mark

> the record of certain accumulations of human achievements; summations of all that is distinguished in man, the most distinguished, as far as we know, that those various ages produced. But those times came to an end leaving those works of art, those poems in their perfection, like complex shells upon a shore. Men lived in those poems as surely as fish lived in the shells we find among the fossils of the past. But they are not there now.[13]

Before *Book V,* Williams (unlike Eliot and Pound, for whom the literary tradition exists in space, not time) held to an historical view of art. In this context, then, it is clear that the library, the museum, acts to keep the poet *from* the city. And it is the city which for Williams is the object of the poem. As he writes in *Book III:*

> The province of the poem is the world.
> When the sun rises, it rises in the poem
> And when it sets darkness comes down
> And the poem is dark   .

In *Book III* what saves the poet from the museum and draws him back into the world? It is the form of the world, the sexual world, in the shape of the black woman, "Beautiful Thing."

But Williams was unable to make the city the province of *Book V,* the only book he left untitled, but which we might dedicate to the care and preservation of the museum. Paterson, that swill hole of democracy, was beyond saving. It could never be transformed into a Tenochtitlan, Williams' early vision of what the ideal American city had once been but could never be again. Williams' extraordinary essay on "The Destruction of Tenochtitlan"[14] (which is written in a prose so charged with emotion as to be poetry) and his 1934 essay entitled "The American Background" together form the clearest—even luminous—statement he ever made about the city (culture). Tenochtitlan is a utopian city, whose people were infinitely gracious, whose ruler daily shared his food (his "natural wealth") with the people, and whose beauty was to be found in its markets of "onions, leeks, watercresses, nasturtium, sorrel, artichokes and golden thistle'' and ''artifices'' woven *into* architecture and clothing, not winnowed *out* as art and put away in a museum. It was a city whose tribe remained in touch with the primal ground and whose leader, Montezuma, was a poet, an American cacique who ''was the very person of their ornate dreams, so delicate, so prismatically colorful, so full of tinkling sounds and rhythms, so tireless of invention.''

Montezuma is the personification of the New World, not Prufrock, says Williams in his Prologue to *Kora in Hell*. Because Montezuma's Tenochtitlan, unlike the industrial Paterson, understood, and understood consummately, that culture is *not a thing, but an act,* not this or that isolated product of the artist but the entire process of adjusting to local conditions, of creating a community, a city, the process in fact of the first four books of *Paterson,* where emphasis is on the poet walking, talking, on art in the making as a way of life. ''The burning need of a culture,'' says Williams in ''The American Background,''

> is not a choice to be made or not made, voluntarily, any more than it can be satisfied by loans. It has to be where it arises, or everything related to the life there ceases. It isn't a thing: it's an act. If it stands still, it is dead. It is the realization of the qualities of a place in relation to the life which occupies it; embracing everything involved, climate, geographic position, relative size, history, other cultures—as well as the character of its sands, flowers, minerals and the condition of knowledge within its borders. It is the act of lifting these things into an ordered and utilized whole which is culture. It isn't something left over afterward. That is the record only. The act is the thing.[15]

The implication is this: in a perfectly realized culture such as that of Tenochtitlan, art is so flawlessly integrated in the city that it disappears as a separate entity. Here the ''pure'' and the ''real'' (or the virgin and the whore, the two elements which Williams so desires to unite in *Book V*) merge. But just as Tenochtitlan collapsed ''to be reënkindled, never, Never, at least, save in spirit''[16] when it was conquered by the Cortez-rude, acquisitive people from Europe, so Paterson scarcely had a chance to develop a culture of its own. The ''local'' was exploited by such federal money-makers as Hamilton and sabotaged by the imposition of a culture purchased from without. And as cities in the United States grew and museums were built by robber barons to assuage their guilt, Williams argues, the spirit of local community progressively disintegrated. Williams believed, in other words, that in the United States there was historically a pernicious relationship between the rise of the city and the founding of its traditional complement, the museum, which in this case housed an imported, not an indigenous culture. And the corrupting nexus between the city and the museum was wealth.

Thus if Williams' purpose in *Paterson* was to make the local universal, to roll up the particulars into a whole, this is one reason why he ultimately failed. Historically he saw that the cards were stacked against him. For his poetics do not include the romantic belief of beholding the world in a grain of sand. The intervening term in his often-repeated tenet "The local is the universal"[17] is *culture,* an indigenous culture, and the process is an historical one: Local yields CULTURE yields universal. But an authentic, articulate culture could not be raised from the grounds of Paterson, polluted as they were by the industry-saturated Passaic. The city could not be made real.

So in *Paterson V* Williams came as close as he ever did to joining other Moderns in building a personal system—call it a mythology—to replace what had been lost in the course of the Nietzschean nineteenth century and the industrially polluted twentieth century. If he did not create a full-blown Yeatsian system, he did propose a kind of utopia to replace his lost Atlantis, the lost city of Tenochtitlan. What was missing in Paterson was the splendid element of social harmony and beauty found in Tenochtitlan or even in the vital music of Juárez, Tenochtitlan corrupted. What was missing was the union between the pure and the real, a union impossible either to find or create in one-dimensional mid-century America. What was missing, in short, was the visionary, for certainly there was more than an abundance of the "real." And the visionary was to be found, Williams concluded, only in art—in, for example, Breughel's painting of the nativity.

But Williams had his own sacred tenet. It was not an Eliotic union of the Christian Father, Son, and Holy Ghost he wished. Nor the Poundian process based upon the teachings of Confucius and resulting in the building of the city of Dioce "now in the mind indestructible." Nor simple Stevensian contact with the real, something he had had all his life. For Williams it was first the union of virgin and whore:

> the Virgin and the Whore, which
> most endures? the world
> of the imagination most endures   :

[V, i]

As we saw in "Asphodel," it is survival and permanence, not the New,[18] that are the values by which Williams swears in *Paterson V*. But they inhere no longer in the "local" marriage, but rather in the world of the imagination, or more precisely, the realm of the imaginary. It is neither the virgin nor the whore "which / most endures," both being defined in terms of time, either by what has *not happened* to them or by what *has happened* to them. It is not the creation of one out of the other, the making of a virgin from a whore, which could be said to describe the process of "Desert Music." It is instead a fusion of the two into one by the force of the imagination. Williams, in other words, abandons the historical world of Paterson for the timeless world of the imagination, which exists outside of it: the museum. Accordingly, his utopia is not a social construct but a personal image: the unicorn.

The union of opposites, the figure from mythology, the alchemical image of the uroboros—this is a strategy completely new to Williams, a class of images totally new to his poetry. If we understand his lifelong poetics as originating from the dictum "no ideas but in things" and read the late poem "Asphodel, That Greeny Flower" as a reversal of this, we see exactly how unprecedented this final stage of his development is. Neither "thing" nor "idea," the unicorn belongs to the realm of the imaginary. Granted, Williams had to locate another solution when he found that in *Paterson* the city could not be made real. Granted, there is a dialectical logic to the change between the first four books and the fifth. If in the first four he wanted to make what was living a sustaining fiction, in the fifth he he wants to give a fiction life. If in *Book III* he destroys the library as the prison house of language, in *Book V* he exalts the living museum. But why did Williams move beyond or reject the "solution," the peace and contentment, he discovered in "Asphodel"? The central images of whore, virgin, and unicorn suggest an answer.

II. SEXUAL POETICS

No man in my country has seen a woman naked and painted her as if he knew anything except that she was naked. No woman in my country is naked except at night. —*Contact*, IV[19]

Of all the major American poets since Whitman, Williams is without question the most sexual of our major poets, consistently so, with abundant evidence ranging from the cover design of the 1920 *Kora in Hell,* which pictures an ovum surrounded by sperm, to the poet Paterson some thirty-odd years later treading the female ground of the park to "kindle" his mind. Williams' poetics—blunt as they are—he himself frames as a sexual poetics. When in his seventies he looked back at his beginnings, he specifically linked his desires for a non-English poetry, a local, American poetry, to sex:

I came to look at poetry from a local viewpoint; I had to find out for myself; I'd had no instruction beyond high school literature. When I was inclined to write poems, I was very definitely an American kid, confident of himself and also independent. From the beginning I felt I was *not* English. If poetry had to be written, I had to do it my own way. It all happened very quickly. Somehow poetry and the female sex were allied in my mind. The beauty of girls seemed the same to me as the beauty of a poem. I knew nothing at all about the sexual approach but I had to do something about it. I did it in the only terms I knew, through poetry.[20]

He was, he disclosed in his 1951 *Autobiography* with the candor and openness he had always displayed toward the matter of sex, "extremely sexual" in his desires. And in that year, which also saw the publication of the fourth book of *Paterson,* he used the present tense: "I am extremely sexual in my desires: I carry them everywhere and at all times." "I think that from that arises the drive which empowers us all."[21] Williams' particular version of sexual psychology was codified as early as the 1910s, elaborated in *In the American Grain* in 1925 and *A Voyage to Pagany* in 1928, and displayed allegorically in *Paterson I–IV.*

In a 1917 issue of the *Egoist* Williams advanced his idiosyncratic version of the Lockean proposition that sense experience is the basis for our knowledge of the world. The male and the female have radically different sense experiences, he states, arguing that the female is naturally in touch with the earth, the ground, the concrete, fact, and that the male, having no direct link of his own with the earth, is naturally given to stargazing and daydreaming. The male, he therefore concludes, is driven by a kind of earth-envy to pursue the female and thereby possess the earth. "Man's only positive connexion with the earth is in the fleeting sex function," he wrote, warning that "either sex must hold to his own psychology or relinquish its sense of reality."[22]

This tragedy, of course, is exactly what Williams believed befell the Puritans, both sexes, and, through them, America. For the Puritans repressed, suppressed, oppressed the right to touch. Touch: the word and theme resound throughout *In the American Grain*. "It is *this* to be *moral:* to be positive, to be peculiar, to be sure, generous, brave—TO MARRY, to *touch*—to give,"[23] proclaims Williams. It is this contact with the ground, the land, the female body of America which the Indian possessed and through which, Williams asserts, the soul grows, the spirit of an individual and a place (whether a city or an entire country) develops. Given this, he argues that the liberation of the Indian residual in every American, the release of passion in every American woman, "might be the opening of wonders, of freedom to 'save the nation.'"[24] He offers Daniel Boone, that "great voluptuary,"[25] as an example of one of the few Americans who discovered America by undergoing the twin processes of discovering its land and the Indian within himself. Boone, says Williams, allowed himself to be driven by the sexual desires which characterize all men. "Because of a descent to the *ground* of his *desires,*" writes Williams, "was Boone's life important and does it still remain loaded with *power—power* to strengthen every form of *energy* that would be *voluptuous, passionate, possessive* in that place which he *opened*" (italics mine).[26]

But most Americans unfortunately followed the example of Washington and the penny-thrifty Franklin, thus neutralizing their native energy with an equal and opposite force of restraint. As a result the country as a whole suffered from a lack of touch. And from lack of touch followed a lack of closeness, a lack of generosity, a fear of embrace, a brittleness of national soul. "From lack of touch, lack of belief,"[27] Williams succinctly sums it up. For what is moral, he believed, grew out of contact with the ground. The two major themes of *In the American Grain*—America's historical repression of "touch" and its need for a culture of its own—are thus causally related. It is through a sexual approach to the concrete, Williams implies, that an authentic culture is created. Moreover it is through a sexual approach to the text, to writing, that a language is born. This is perhaps seen most clearly in *A Voyage to Pagany* where Williams describes Evans who "made a wife of his writing, his writing—that desire to free himself from his besetting reactions by transcending them—thus driving off his torments and going often to sleep thereafter."[28]

Not surprisingly, it is this twin process which Williams chose as the rather crude allegorical structure for *Paterson I–IV*. Paterson, male, doctor and writer, personifies the city. The park, female, personifies the ground, both the land and the body. And the predictable problem is to bring the two together in a satisfying manner. The problem is to give real voice to the thoughts (the people) of Paterson:

> Who because they
> neither know their sources nor the sills of their
> disappointments walk outside their bodies aimlessly
> for the most part,
> locked and forgot in their desires—unaroused.
>
> [I, i]

To arouse the people, that is the problem. But as the poem progresses nothing could seem less probable. *Book I:* "The Delineaments of the Giants" pictures Paterson youth as sexually immature:

> —unfledged desire, irresponsible, green,
> colder to the hand than stone,
> unready—challenging our waking:
>
> [I, ii]

Book II: "Sunday in the Park" is an anti-Seurat scene of flagrant desire and frustration. "Frank vulgarity" is the best that can be expected from the working classes, what with some men too fat and flaccid to move even a minor muscle and others unaroused and worse, unaware of the impulse of desire itself. By *Book IV:* "The Run to the Sea," the decay of healthy sexual relationships has spread to the upper classes. In the lesbian scenes ironically titled "An Idyl," Williams exposes sex as not just abortive or unrealized, but as unnatural. And it is either this, he implies, or nothing at all. For in the city, in the financial district, the people are completely stripped, "unsexed":

> At the
> sanitary lunch hour packed woman to
> woman (or man to woman, what's the difference?)
> the flesh of their faces gone
> to fat or gristle, without recognizable
> outline, fixed in rigors, adipose or sclerosis
> expressionless, facing one another, a mould
> for all faces (canned fish) this
>
> [IV, i]

Yet throughout the first four books of *Paterson* Williams does present a model of a healthy sexual being who falters only once or twice, and that is Paterson (Williams) himself. There is no need to detail this since each and every page could stand as document. Paterson? "His mind drinks of desire." Let it suffice to point out that Paterson's explicitly sexual sensibility is revealed in his countless images of flowers and tongues of bees, pubic groves of trees, and pearl grey towers. In his sensitivity to the land (female) upon which he "instructs" his thoughts, focusing his mind on the concrete, on for example the recurrent, rhythmic, flaming flight of grasshoppers from which he again realizes that there is "no flesh but the caress!" In the letters from "C" which expose his sexual (if not sexist) approach to the text, or it could be said, his textual approach to sex. And finally in the scenes in which Williams dramatizes Paterson's actual physical involvement with women—in Paterson's insisting, in fact shouting, that the black girl he calls "Beautiful Thing" take off her clothes ("let me purify myself," he says), or in *Book IV,* Paterson's effort, though unsuccessful, to seduce the very young and somewhat virginal nurse Phyllis in his office.

With his sexual orientation to the world, Paterson is entirely unlike

the personae Stevens and Eliot chose for themselves in their profoundly personal late poems.

> Sing me a song to make death tolerable, a song
> of a man and a woman: the riddle of a man
> and a woman,

says Williams in *Book III*. Such a song, sexual and stronger than any
in *Book V,* appears in *Book I*. It is Williams' version of the still point:

> We sit and talk,
> quietly, with long lapses of silence
> and I am aware of the stream
> that has no language, coursing
> beneath the quiet heaven of
> your eyes
>
>   which has no speech; to
> go to bed with you, to pass beyond
> the moments of meeting, while the
> currents float still in mid-air, to
> fall—
> with you from the brink, before
> the crash—
>
>   to seize the moment.
>
> We sit and talk, sensing a little
> the rushing impact of the giant's
> violent torrent rolling over us, a
> few moments.
>
>   If I should demand it, as
> it has been demanded of others
> and given too swiftly, and you should
> consent. If you would consent
>
>   We sit and talk and the
> silence speaks of the giants
> who have died in the past and have
> returned to those scenes unsatisfied
> and who is not unsatisfied, the
> silent, Singac the rock-shoulder

> emerging from the rocks—and the giants
> live again in your silence and
> unacknowledged desire—
> And the air lying over the water
> lifts the ripples, brother
> to brother, touching as the mind touches. . . .
>
> [I, ii]

If Eliot could reach this peak of ineffable experience, a point where all
time is stopped, only through the rhythms of abstract language,
Williams can reach it only through the body, through sex, through the
union of male with female. Suspended beyond the world, beyond the
need for language and the desire for speech, Williams discovers in this
silence that the giants of the past live again.

At first this might appear a contradiction of Williams' much talked
about mission in *Paterson* to invent the exact language to evoke the
people, an American idiom to find the rhythm of Paterson life. And it
would be if Williams' search were interpreted, as it often is, on the
level of poetic technique—the variable foot et al.—and on that level
only. But Williams was not so narrow a man. In *Paterson* he wanted
also to dramatize the need for touch, for as we've seen it was from this
that a culture could be created. The touch of the mind must be sensual:

> And the air lying over the water
> lifts the ripples, brother
> to brother, touching as the mind touches. . . .

The process is this: from the sexual (sensual, local) to the cultural, to
the universal.

III. THE WOMAN IN THE MIND INDESTRUCTIBLE

> Old men cut from touch.
>
> "The Old Men"[29]

If the Williams of *Paterson I–IV*, a man in his mid-sixties, were to
be described, one would characterize him as a lusty old man. If one of
the questions he asked himself was

> Doctor, do you believe in
> "the people," the Democracy? Do

> you still believe—in this
> swill-hole of corrupt cities?
> Do you, Doctor? Now?
>
>   [III, i]

the answer he gave throughout those four books was, on balance, yes. Yes, *he* could embrace, desired to embrace, women, even though, in fact *because,* they did not embody classical (European) beauty. Their beauty was in defiance of authority, a quality Williams had singled out in "The American Background" as being quintessentially American.[30] And yes, because at the end of *Book IV* Williams in spite of it all could still head inland, toward other centers of culture. Yes, in short, because Williams in *Paterson I–IV* had a sexual hold on life.

But if we were to ask this same question of the Williams of *Paterson V,* we would have to answer no, he does not still believe in that swill-hole, now he wants to "avoid / the irreverent." Whereas in *Book II* he had enjoined himself to "Be reconciled, poet, with your world, it is / the only truth!," now he insists upon embracing other less tangible worlds, other centuries. And if we were to characterize him now it would be as the wise old man reminiscent of the elder Eliot, Pound, and Stevens, a calm figure who seeks to preserve and hand on tradition. Before Willimas had instructed young writers to "write carelessly so that nothing that is not green will survive." Now he sees himself as imparting courage, answers, and his own tradition in order

> to get the young
>   to foreshorten
> their errors in the use of words which
> he had found so difficult, the errors
> he had made in the use of the
> poetic line
>
>   [V, iii]

Why this change? Because the link between the body and the mind, sex and the text, had been snapped. And with the loss of touch, Williams lost his American background. He says as much in *I Wanted to Write a Poem,* published the very year *Paterson V* was published:

> ... *Paterson V* must be written, is being written.... Why must it be written? *Paterson IV* ends with the protagonist breaking through the bushes, identifying himself with the land, with America. He finally will die but it can't be categorically stated that death ends *anything*. When you're through with sex, with ambition, what can an old man create? Art, of course, a piece of art that will go beyond him into the lives of young people, the people who haven't had time to create. The old man meets the young people and lives on.[31]

"When you're through with sex, with ambition, what must an old man create?" We must not be hesitant to take this literally, for Williams was a very literal-minded man. Accordingly, the opening lines of *Paterson V* do not so much express a breakthrough for the poet, as they rather frame this very problem:

> In old age
>
>   the mind
>
>   casts off
>   rebelliously
>   an eagle
> from its crag
>
>   —the angle of a forehead
>   or far less
>   makes him remember when he thought
>   he had forgot
>
>   —remember
>
>   confidently
>   only a moment, only for a fleeting moment—
>   with a smile of recognitions . .
>
>   [V, i]

For some readers Williams is now triumphant, "less bound by his locality and his immediate present"; he now is free "from time and place."[32] But when had Williams ever desired this? I read the passage this way: in old age, his old age, writes Williams, the mind attempts to rebel from the body, the rock which represents the poem. And it is a rebellion nearly successful because the body is almost completely passive, *but* fortunately a physical sign will occasionally restore himself to himself. The very problem, in other words, is that his mind is no longer stirred by actual contact, by touch, by sex, but only by experience once removed—memory. The problem is a collapse of his world. The flesh of the female, the one indispensable element in his way of being in and with the world, has been removed.

How to define himself? How to adjust? A curious kind of narcissism confronts him:

> —shall we speak of love
> seen only in a mirror
> —no replica?
> reflecting only her impalpable spirit?
> which is she whom I see
> and not touch her flesh?
>
> [V, iii]

The mood is that of melancholy, elegy. As he unsentimentally characterizes himself,

> Paterson has grown older
>
> the dog of his thoughts
> has shrunk
> to no more than "a passionate letter"
> to a woman, a woman he had neglected
> to put to bed in the past
>
> [V, iii]

Much less neglect to put to bed, worse, he does not even manage to ask the name of his "Solitary Reaper," his "To the One of Fictive Music," the plain woman he sees in the streets. What does he want of himself? "Paterson, / keep your pecker up / whatever the detail!" What does he wish? He includes the long letter from G. S. telling in rushing, drunk-high prose about the whore in all-white, the virgin, bride, but this is no longer a part of his life. He translates a poem of Sappho's but "a delicate fire" no longer runs through his veins.

What he desires is desire itself. What he wants is a vision. "The dream / is in pursuit!" he says, and although he is here referring to the making of an artist, the lines sum up *his* need as well. He needs a new goal—and he defines it as the element of splendor. Or, to read the situation somewhat differently, he needs *to be* pursued. No longer able *to possess*, no longer active as he was in *Paterson I–IV*, now he wants *to be* possessed. But he has retired from the world of people. In the world of the first four books his dreams were the people themselves. Now he asserts:

> Dreams possess me
> > and the dance
> > > of my thoughts
> > involve animals
> > > the blameless beasts.

> > > > > > > [V, ii]

And in the third and final section of *Book V* he observes in the calm tone of the third person that "Though he is approaching / death he is possessed by many poems." To be possessed by dreams, by art, that is his desire. Desire, we might say, is in *Book V* (dis)placed in art. The calm he experiences, we might say, is not so much a finding of a balance he had never had, but a way of achieving a dynamic equilibrium he had once had with the world and lost. Since neither of his two models of perfection—that of Tenochtitlan on the social level, or that of the still point on the sexual level—are possible, he creates a substitute: the imaginary.

Williams thus moves from the "hot" society of *Paterson I–IV* where meaningful human exchange is defined for him in sexual terms (if not for the other characters)[33] to the "cold" society of *Paterson V*, inhabited by himself, a few letter writers, a few works of art, and a few, only a few, memories (Williams is not given to much nostalgia here), and initially empty of the Woman he must create in order to create a role for himself.

In *Book V* he finds himself turning to tradition for models, or at least inspiration, because, following Pound's economic theories, in times past, there was local control of purchasing power. As he puts it, shorthand, in *Book IV*, "Difference between squalor of spreading slums / splendor of renaissance cities." The Renaissance? It stretches for him from at least the twelfth century (the century he attributes to the

fifteenth-century Cloister tapestries in which he imagines the people
"All together, working together") to the seventeenth, to Brueghel's
three wise men who "had eyes for visions / in those days." And so did
Brueghel, who knew what Williams found himself just learning, or just
needing:

> Peter Brueghel the artist saw it
> from the two sides the
> imagination must be served—
> and he served
>
>   dispassionately
>
>   [V, iii]

Until *Book V,* if I may simplify, Williams had been concerned with
one side only, the real. Now confronted with death (which on one level
was very certainly the death of desire) Williams needed a living fiction. The triumph of his imagination was this: not to invest a few past
masterpieces with life by showing just how concrete they were,[34] but to
work with traditional image clusters in a way unknown to him before
and create from them a new language of the self within which he could
survive. If before his was an unmediated vision, now he found it
necessary to devise a system, or at the very least, assert a belief to
stand between himself and both the world he could no longer touch and
approaching death. Interpreted this way, the development of his poetic
career is seen to be the very reverse of that of Wallace Stevens, who
spent a lifetime *imagining* reality and only at the very end made the
American breakthrough to perceiving the blunt edge of the thing itself.
Like Stevens' concept of the imagination, Williams' "system" is not
so much a strategy for putting himself in contact with the world of
particulars—it does not act at all as a pipeline to the concrete—as it is a
way of allowing the imagination to exert an equal pressure on the now
intolerable force of reality, intolerable because it was either too much
with him in the shape of death, or intolerable because it was not
enough with him in the shape of sex. The imaginary is a way, we could
say, of countervailing the all-too-sharp reality principle.

The three central images—virgin/whore, unicorn, and the
uroboros—are distinctly related: the first two form an idiosyncratic

religious symbol from which, we could say, the uroboros, a figure of wholeness, can be generated. Williams' desire, announced in the first section of *Book V,* is to build a "secret world" so that he can "get to the end of the sphere." In the third and final section he asserts that he has done just that:

> The (self) direction has been changed
>   the serpent
>   its tail in its mouth
> "the river has returned to its beginnings"
>   and backward
>   (and forward)
>   it tortures itself within me
>   until time has been washed finally under:
>   and "I knew all (or enough)
>   it became me   .   "
>
>   [V, iii]

In *Book IV* Williams presented us with a modern-day industrial equivalent of the virgin/whore in the uneducated, unscrupulous, teasing Phyllis, who, it is clear, is qualified to be taken for a virgin and damned a whore, but for precisely the wrong reasons. As a counterpart to Phyllis, in *Book V* he postulates an ideal synthesis of the virgin/whore—that of mistress/wife—through a characteristic Williams mixture of the traditions of Christianity, courtly love, and Toulouse-Lautrec. *Book V* is dedicated to Toulouse-Lautrec because, as Williams observed in *Book III,*

> Toulouse Lautrec witnessed
> it: Limbs relaxed
> —all religions
>   have excluded it—
> at ease, the tendons
> untensed   .
>
>   [III, i]

Williams' "religion," however, does include it—the sexual. For Williams, the virgin/whore unites both the innocent and the seductive in a sacred union. The virtuous woman gives herself like a gift, unhesitantly, to her lover, as does the ideal whore. And the ideal whore is a virgin, and the ideal virgin, Mary, mother and whore of the Holy Ghost. This virgin/whore is a purely imaginary construct. Since sex is no longer an affair of the body, it must exist in the mind:

> —every married man carries in his head
> the beloved and sacred image
> of a virgin
>
> whom he has whored   .
>
> [V, iii]

In this vision Williams identifies himself with the unicorn, legendary touchstone of virgins and long established symbol of Christ, a fabulous, solitary, ferocious, gentle, beautiful, melancholy, magical creature.[35] We can assume that Williams chose the unicorn—which legend tells us appears freely only to wise men and is tamed only by virgins—as symbol for himself and the artist, as well as the symbol of what he himself pursued, because the unicorn, "la licorne," is both "dame" and "demoiselle," both whore and virgin, virginal in its whiteness and power of purification and whorelike in its possession of the horn. In French tradition the unicorn, although androgynous, is thus considered essentially feminine, an incarnation of the multivalent nature of woman. But Williams diverges from this tradition by casting the unicorn as male, thereby merging three in one in a new-found trinity, itself an image of wholeness, a virile analogue to the uroboros. In the unicorn, Williams thus finds an image for what was only a hypothesis in *Book III* ("Say I am the locus / where two women meet") and fulfills a dream of *Book IV:*

> To bring himself in,
> hold together wives in one wife and
> at the same time scatter it,
> the one in all of them   .
>
> Weakness,
> weakness dogs him, fulfillment only
> a dream or in a dream.
>
> [IV, iii]

Thus from out of his long-held theory of the sexual origin of the text (whether it be a poem or a person, a city or a culture), in *Paterson V* Williams turns to the corollary that art is both male and female and constructs an imaginary set to mediate between a diminished life and a coming death. From this point, theoretically he can re-member, re-turn, re-awaken. Now his world can come round again: "The (self) direction has been changed." Although trapped, penned-up, and penned-in, he can face the "aging body," for he lives in a safe and secret world of symbols which "rolls back into the past":

> Through this hole
> at the bottom of the cavern
> of death, the imagination
> escapes intact.

[V, i]

In the fifth book of *Paterson* then, the poem becomes for Williams a personal instrument in a way that it had never been before. As late as 1950 he had defined the poem as having a social function. As he said then, "The poem to me (until I go broke) is an attempt, an experiment, a failing experiment, toward assertion with broken means but an assertion, always, of a new and total culture, the lifting of an environment to expression. Thus it is social, the poem is a social instrument—accepted or not accepted seems to be of no material importance."[36] But in *Paterson V* the poem becomes first and foremost a means of personal salvation, not a vehicle for raising an American culture.

In *Book III* Williams had prophesied *Book V*:

> The descent beckons
>   as the ascent beckoned
>   Memory is a kind
> of accomplishment
>   a sort of renewal
>   even
> an initiation, since the spaces it opens are new
> places
>
>   .   .

[III, iii]

New spaces, new places—this is just what Williams makes in *Book V*. But the form this memory takes is not so much the memories of his own past—for these are few and fleeting as he himself admits. Nor I

would suggest, is it the larger field of the unconscious, although the
unicorn and uroboros are indeed what we have come to call archetypal
symbols. Rather this "memory" is that of Western consciousness
objectified in European art from which Williams borrows a goal (the
inclusion of the element of "splendor," I have called it) and adopts,
adapts a set of images for his own use. As I suggested earlier, this
strategy sounds curiously like what Williams had accused Pound and
Eliot of in *Book I*—of running off

> toward the peripheries—
> to other centers, direct—
> for clarity (if
> they found it)
> > loveliness and
> authority in the world—
>
> > > > [I, iii]

And it is. But Williams' understanding of what Pound and Eliot were
doing was meager. If we compare the Williams of *Paterson V* with the
Pound of the *Pisan Cantos,* the Eliot of the *Four Quartets,* and the
Stevens of *The Rock,* we understand just how much his poem suffers in
comparison.

As we have seen, the impulse of the long, meditative poem among
these American poets is to find what will suffice in old age, or, as in
the case of Eliot, what can be projected for an old age. And as a form it
is impressive, primarily because its successes are hard won over a long
period of poetic practice, but also because the emphasis is on process
and becoming. Process: this by now has become a commonplace of
criticism, but we must not let familiarity harden us to what should
remain fresh. The meditative poem has a hidden dramatic form, and
for this reason, insights can be revealed which are persuasive,
moments can "occur" which are similar to Joycean epiphanies.

In *Paterson V* this is missing. For if Williams intended to adopt the
meditative mode of the Stevens of *The Rock* and the Eliot of the *Four
Quartets,* as indeed his allusions suggest and his age required, it is
clear that he either did not understand it or his long life in poetry had
not prepared him for an entirely new way of writing. Certainly the

meditative mode was new to him. Earlier he had most often structured his poems in simple terms of anecdote ("This Is Just To Say," for example), portraiture ("Sympathetic Portrait of a Child"), the image ("Spouts") and/or combinations of the three, which tended to result in a fleshing out of the narrative line, upon which *Paterson I–IV,* however much it may look on the page like a modern collage, is bedrock built. Nor did "Asphodel, That Greeny Flower" provide him with experience in the strategy of the meditative poem (no matter how much we wish to be genuinely, not sentimentally, moved by it), being as it is a rather flaccid amble down an associational memory lane:

> And so
> > with fear in my heart
> > > I drag it out
> And keep on talking
> > for I dare not stop.

But *Paterson V* falls into none of these categories. Williams drops the structural methods of the narrative and association and substitutes—what? What is the process by which he would win the discovery of the uroboros, symbol of integrations, wholeness? Although the reader can point to an Eliotic question in section one of *Paterson V* and an Eliotic assertion in section three, it is much more difficult to locate an underlying dramatic or rhetorical logic which allows Williams to make this affirmation. The truth is this—that Williams does not so much experience as assert. His purpose was dramatic, but he could not escape the tyranny of the object. In *Paterson V* he continued his old habit of description: he chose a brilliantly defined object—the tapestry which weaves the narrative of the unicorn—for his symbol, not something ineffable, irreducible to an object, such as Eliot's notion of the still point.

In *I Wanted to Write a Poem* Williams said that those people who had accused him of writing antipoetry had prophesied that "when I have suffered . . . I too shall run for cover; that I too shall seek refuge in fantasy. And mind you, I do not say that I will not. To decorate my age."[37] It would not be too outrageous to suggest that this is indeed just what he does in *Paterson V*—that he decorates a substitute world with unicorns and flowers and a grim reaper and serpents gripping their tales in their mouths as though they were so many paintings to be hung on the wall of the text. There is something, in other words, curiously unconvincing about *Paterson V,* and Louis Martz's definition of the goal (not the procedure) of meditative poetry helps us understand what it is. For Martz the meditative poet "seeks himself in himself in order to discover or to construct a firm position from which he can include the universe."[38] Williams, cut off from his lifelong concept of himself, divorced from the ground (the sexual) and thus divorced from his native culture (the American grain), sought himself outside himself, never reaching a still point from which he could include the universe. This was his failure, but his courage was also in this: the infirmities of age demanded that he do what he had not done before, and confronting those weaknesses, he invented something new.

1. William Carlos Williams, *I Wanted to Write a Poem,* ed. Edith Heal (New York: Beacon Press, 1958), p. 38.

2. Letter from William Carlos Williams to Louis Martz, May 27, 1951, in *The Selected Letters of William Carlos Williams,* ed. John C. Thirwall (New York: McDowell, Obolensky, 1957), p. 298.

3. See, for example, Sherman Paul, *The Music of Survival: A Biography of a Poem by William Carlos Williams* (Urbana: University of Illinois Press, 1968).

4. William Carlos Williams, "The American Background," *Selected Essays of William Carlos Williams* (New York: New Directions, 1969), p. 142.

5. William Carlos Williams, *Pictures from Brueghel and Other Poems* (New York: New Directions, 1962). This volume also contains the poems of *The Desert Music* and *Journey to Love.*

6. Jerome Mazzaro's *William Carlos Williams: The Later Poems* (Ithaca: Cornell University Press, 1973) is a superbly researched, impressively thorough, and clearly written full-length study of Williams' late poems. Given the time lags between research, writing, and publication, I must confess that I had not read Mazzaro's book at the time I conceived this chapter. It must be clear to any reader familiar with his book that we have much in common. Mazzaro's study links "the phenomenal world of the older writer with the dreams he had in his youth"; in addition, we both agree that "the line between artistic form and life in Williams . . . often blurred" and therefore need not be obsessively dealt with as a thorny theoretical problem. I refer the reader especially to Mazzaro's fascinating work on the figure of the wise old man in Williams' writing and his chapter on the relationship in Williams between sex and writing.

7. Letter to Flexmore Hudson, *Briarcliff Quarterly,* 3 (October 1946), 205–8.

8. *Selected Essays,* pp. 142–43.

9. See, for example, Joseph Riddel's brilliant study of Williams entitled *The Inverted Bell: Modernism and the Counterpoetics of William Carlos Williams* (Baton Rouge: Louisiana State University Press, 1974). Riddel argues that *Paterson V* is the discourse of the method of *Paterson* ("that consummate metapoem in Williams' canon" [p. 35]). For Riddel, the figure of the virgin and the whore represents the poet's act of naming. But here I see a problem. Riddel interprets the counterpoetics of Williams as inhering in his recognition that we must abandon the search for authority (which Riddel understands as the lost center, presence, the origin, plenitude), and thus he understands the unicorn's pursuit of the virgin as one that is consistently thwarted and "must repeatedly involve itself in a violation of the object it desires—the inevitable whoring of the virgin" (p. 260). But when was this violence disagreeable or lamentable to Williams? The pursuit, it seems more likely to me, is of women, not the Word, the missing center. The problem here is raising every image to a level of abstraction which the text can not persuasively carry.

10. "Prologue to *Kora in Hell,*" in *Selected Essays,* p. 21.

11. "Prologue to *Kora in Hell,*" in *Selected Essays,* p. 24.

12. "Preface," *Selected Essays,* n.p.

13. "An Approach to the Poem," in *English Institute Essays* (New York: Columbia University Press, 1948), p. 55.

14. William Carlos Williams, "The Destruction of Tenochtitlan," in *In the American Grain* (New York: New Directions, 1956).

15. *Selected Essays,* p. 157.

16. "The Destruction of Tenochtitlan," in *In the American Grain,* p. 32.

17. "Introduction to Charles Sheeler—Paintings—Drawings—Photographs," in *Selected Essays,* p. 233.

18. Williams could be said to be a forerunner of the Tradition of the New. See his "Prologue to *Kora in Hell,*" in *Selected Essays,* p. 21: "Nothing is good save the new. If a Thing have novelty it stands intrinsically beside every other work of artistic excellence. If it have not that, no loveliness or heroic proportion or grand manner will save it."

19. *Selected Essays,* p. 31.

20. *I Wanted to Write a Poem,* p. 14.

21. *The Autobiography of William Carlos Williams* (New York: Random House, 1951), p. 311.

22. William Carlos Williams, "Correspondence: The Great Sex Spiral," *The Egoist,* 4 (August 1917), 110–11.

23. *In the American Grain,* p. 121.

24. *In the American Grain,* p. 185.

25. *In the American Grain,* p. 130.

26. *In the American Grain,* p. 136.

27. *In the American Grain,* p. 128.

28. William Carlos Williams, *A Voyage to Pagany* (New York: The Macaulay Co., 1928), pp. 145–46.

29. William Carlos Williams, *The Collected Early Poems of William Carlos Williams* (New York: New Directions, 1951), p. 158.

30. As he wrote in "In the American Background," in *Selected Essays,* p. 143: "One might go on to develop the point from this that the American addition to world culture will always be the 'new,' in opposition to an 'old' represented by Europe. But that isn't satisfactory. What is actually is something much deeper: a relation to the immediate conditions of the matter in hand, and a determination to assert them in opposition to all intermediate authority. Deep in the pattern of the newcomers' minds was impressed that conflict between present reliance on the prevalent conditions of place and the overriding of an unrelated authority."

31. *I Wanted to Write a Poem,* p. 26.

32. See, for example, Walter Sutton's "Dr. Williams' *Paterson* and the Quest for Form," in *The Merrill Studies in Paterson,* ed. John Engels (Columbus, Ohio: Charles E. Merrill, 1971), p. 55.

33. This identifies one of the basic structural weaknesses of *Paterson 1–IV.* Williams characterizes Paterson the man and poet as being sexually aware and aggressive, but describes Paterson the city as being the opposite.

34. See Louis Martz, "The Unicorn in *Paterson:* William Carlos Williams," *Thought,* 35 (Winter 1960), 537–54.

35. See Bertrand d'Astorg's *Le Mythe de la Dame à la Licorne* (Paris: Editions aux Seuil, 1963), and the Metropolitan Museum of Art's publication entitled *The Unicorn Tapestries at the Cloisters* (New York: Metropolitan Museum of Art, 1946).

36. Letter from William Carlos Williams to Henry Wells, April 12, 1950, in *Selected Letters,* p. 286.

37. *I Wanted to Write a Poem,* p. 38.

38. *The Poem of the Mind,* p. 31.

6

The Sense of an Ending

One of the central concerns of this book is the nature of wisdom. This is a question that deeply interests me, in part because wisdom is so little valued in today's technological society. Generally speaking, wisdom is confused with authoritarianism and dismissed as specious, rather than identified with the persuasiveness of right ideas, that is, authority (it is difficult even to rescue the word "authority" from contempt). In the Introduction I refer to Gregory Bateson's definition of wisdom as he conceives it in *Steps Toward an Ecology of Mind*. There he writes of wisdom as the understanding of "the larger interactive system—that system which if disturbed, is likely to generate exponential curves of change." For Bateson wisdom is an understanding of the pattern which connects a system. The metaphors he uses are derived from both ecology and information theory; in terms of a cultural system, he believes, wisdom is crucial to health and social stability (not stagnation). In some of the societies Bateson has studied, such an understanding of the pattern which connects a system—its interdependencies—is built into cultural practices unconsciously. But as any intelligent critic of contemporary industrial society knows, this is not the case in our culture. We are introducing change into our culture—and those of others—so rapidly that it cannot be absorbed; explosive curves of change are being generated which threaten to destroy the system itself. Given this crisis, what is necessary for our culture is a conscious, not unconscious, perspective on the whole which is actively learned. Although in the text I quoted above Bateson is speaking primarily about a cultural system, we can apply his ideas to the idea of an individual life as well. The problem can then be reformulated: What is the connection between the crisis in our culture and old age? What is the relationship between action and a certain quality of thoughtfulness?

For me, wisdom is intuitively connected with age, hence this book. Why? Is there a necessary, although not sufficient, connection between wisdom and age? (I recognize, of course, that we can speak of a young man as wise and that by this, we generally mean he is balanced in his judgments; the wisdom of Stevens' Penelope, as I have shown, differs from this. When we refer to a man in his late seventies as youthful, I suspect we mean that he is still active in the conventional sense, while the wise old man is characterized by a certain stasis, a lack of overt movement. In our culture there is no question that we tend to value the former over the latter, as we value action over reflectiveness.) In the poems considered here, age does bring perspective, a vision of the whole which is possible only from a summit. The problematics of perspective—of the relationship between action and quietism, experience and meaning—pervades, as we have seen, much of the *Four Quartets:* Eliot was not sure whether he was indeed old or not. On the other hand, we find this constituting perspective transparently articulated in Stevens' last poems—a global view of his life before him, his poems a planet on his table. The old man must be poised in a tower, as Yeats also knew, nowhere else.

If this is so, the perspective is not to be identified with action. For action requires partisanship, an embodiment of a point of view within the system rather than a perspective on the whole of the system, even when one understands that others may have competing, equally valid claims (believing that a system is sustained by countervailing powers is not wise). Perhaps this is one reason why Stevens finally relinquished his hold on the idea of a supreme fiction. Action and wisdom are basically antithetical, although we surely can speak of a wise action or a wisdom that is not passive. If they are antithetical, we see how the wisdom of the aged plays its traditional role in a time which requires it more urgently than ever before: the image of the wise old man relieves the pressure to action, and, for the time being, it is my guess that the less we "do" in terms of introducing change into our system, the better.

But, as I have shown, the model of a wise relationship to the world is much more subtle than a self-conscious halt to action. The meditative mode, as it is exemplified by both Stevens' Penelope and Santayana, represents an easy interpenetration between mind and world which is achieved by surrendering a large measure of self-consciousness; the unity between mind and nature in Stevens' "World as Meditation" represents a system functioning harmoniously of its own accord.

How is such a perspective achieved? Again, I refer to Bateson, whose recent *Mind and Nature: A Necessary Unity,* published when he was seventy-five, further develops his theory of the ecological evolution of mind. The last sentence of his book poses a question which he originally addressed to the Regents of the University of California: "As *teachers,*" he asks, "are we wise?" To convey what he means by wisdom, Bateson evokes the image of the still point. "The still point is the setting of the turning world,"[1] he writes in a discussion of the differences between "feedback" and "calibration," two modes of attaining a connection one desires with the world. To illustrate the two processes, Bateson uses the examples of shooting a rifle and firing a shotgun, respectively. In the former, he notes, the marksman does not carry forward what he has learned from one shot to the next, whereas in the latter the opposite is true: success is based on learning from past experience. "The rifleman simply goes round his cybernetic circuit a number of *separate* times; the man with a shotgun must accumulate his skill, packing his successive experiences, like Chinese boxes, each within the context of information derived from all previous relevant experiences."[2]

This we can relate to the kind of learning achieved within the life span of an artist. Working with a problem over a long period of time—a particular form, a certain theme—an artist embodies the very process of calibration (this is not to be confused with simple experience or short-term problem solving; tackling one problem and then another and then another is not the same as persisting in a single-minded effort over a long period of time). In just this way, the achievement of these poets—all extraordinarily gifted men—has been the result of a long life in poetry, the fruit of the exacting demands of shaping language to fit their needs and visions. Working with a material, meeting its resistances with one's own ideas, this is a learning process, a form of what Bateson calls calibration. It is also what we call mastering a discipline, combining rigor with imagination, and as such it does not come about spontaneously, magically, automatically. Whereas in these poems the model of correct thought—what I have called the meditative mode—presupposes a relaxing of the mind, an ecological balance between mind and world that is appropriate to the age of the poets and the requirements of our age, this possibility was prepared only by an active shaping of language, the raw material. This learning must be won, it is not merely granted. There is no contradiction here. One of the themes dramatized in these poems is that of creative readiness for the unexpected moment, a receptivity to experience, which has been prepared by a long process of learning about the relationship between the self and the world, the mind and the world. Without this, the condition of receptivity to experience could be too easily mistaken for passivity.

Moreover, certainly the poems themselves are products of thought, forms which have been made. Indeed the implied tension between the two poles—the condition of receptivity to experience and the active shaping of words—may be disturbing, for in some cases the tension is so great that the "next" poem, the possibility or even the necessity of the act of writing, threatens to collapse under the strain. Both Eliot and Stevens, I sense, moved toward *not* writing. Eliot, as we know, did indeed stop writing poetry. And for Stevens simply *to be* seems at times to be enough. As he wrote in 1950 in a moving letter, which I quoted earlier, "It is not always easy to tell the difference between thinking and looking out of the window." To write or not to write. As critics, we find the very question shocking. Why should it disturb us so? Stevens gives us an image of stillness, not stagnation. Perhaps the *production* of meaning itself is no longer necessary. To again quote Bateson: "To be still is the essence of calibration. The still point is the setting of the turning world."

To be still and yet moving: a symbol of wisdom. In all four of these poets, this paradox—the impetus of movement finding its source in stillness—is reflected in yet another way which is in itself an astonishing achievement. Their wisdom is revealed in their ability to incorporate change into the body of their poetry. In confronting the limit to what the self can achieve—death (I except Eliot)—they understood wisdom to be a reaching beyond one's strength. And in the process they found new strengths. Their poetry suggests that over time one's art can be a self-correcting system, as I put it earlier. The act of writing is, as Wallace Stevens wrote so enigmatically and eloquently in "The Rock",

> ... a cure of ourselves, that is equal to a cure
> Of the ground, a cure beyond forgetfulness.

For each poet, what had to be given up and what embraced are different, conditioned by private obsessions. It is as if they intuitively understood that they had work which could only be finished by an act of balancing. In the *Four Quartets* Eliot did what he could to reach beyond the impersonality of the poet—one of his preoccupations—to present himself, the personal. Stevens had to silence the incessant meta-poetry of the mind, abandon the dream of the supreme fiction, and accept the thing itself; he desired "reconciliation with every-day reality." "The trouble is that poetry," he wrote, "is so largely a matter of transformation. To describe a cup of tea without changing it and without concerning oneself with some extreme aspect of it is not at all the easy thing that it seems to be."[3] In the *Pisan Cantos* Pound moved beyond the elite sphere of "literary" history and into the world of outcast men, and magnificently united the two. And Williams made the most ambitious effort of the four. For Williams the natural object had always been both necessary and sufficient, but in the whole of *Paterson* he abandoned imagism for allegory and abstraction, and in the fifth book he exchanged the industrial ground of the United States for the European tradition of art. He was wise to do this, although the radical difference between the two histories was too great for him to bridge.

The integration of the "new" or the "other" in these poems lends support to a developmental theory of psychology. Again, it is not the case that the poems and poets verify the theory or vice versa. Nor do I subscribe by temperament to the mystical metaphors we find in Jungian psychology or Neumann's work. Furthermore, I think it is wise to heed Nisbet's warning that we be suspicious of organic metaphors which imply growth and progress, when in fact there may be only change. But Nisbet's insight is particularly useful only when it is applied to the development of society. Certainly we need to question the myth of progress and trace the intellectual roots of this mistaken analysis, but what is curious is that for centuries we should have obsessively applied the metaphor of growth to society—a nonorganic construct—and denied it to individuals. This is a perversity in our thinking, which perhaps the system has exacted from us for its own growth: industrial society required economic man who, when old, could be discarded because he was no longer useful. But it is not accurate to think about the development of a society and the development of an individual in the same terms. To do so is to make an error in what Bateson calls logical types (Eliot understood this).

And yet the resistance on the part of the intellectual community to developmental psychology is tenacious. Why is this so? I suggest the hostility masks a fear of growing old. We reject the very possibility of development for it requires that we accept change and ultimately death. The psychological mechanism at work is familar: one denies value to that which one fears, thus keeping it at arm's length. But this is complicated. What we deny to others, we also partially accord to ourselves, not realizing that this involves us in a contradiction, a blindness to our own future. Our everyday experience of our *own* lives tells us that we grow wiser as we grow older. Most of us have a sense of personal growth, most of us would not wish to repeat our lives, most of us believe that we do accumulate experience. Yet we tend not to perceive this in others. Nor do we associate it with old age. *Others* are old, *we* are not. This fear of old age may be so deep that it is coeval with consciousness itself, rooted in awareness of our own mortality, which we steadfastly deny. As Simone de Beauvoir has written: "Whatever the context may be, the biological facts remain. For every individual age brings with it a dreaded decline. . . . Old age in others also causes an instant repulsion. This primitive reaction remains alive even when custom represses it; and in this we see the origin of a conflict that we shall find exemplified again and again."[4] Thus the wisdom of these four poets inheres in their having recognized, and accepted, the "other," what was always the stranger to their work, the ghost, the image of themselves as old, mutability. They asserted a connection between age and wisdom. To quote Herbert Blau: "All is still at the still point of the turning wheel. The circular movement activates all the dark and light forces of human nature. Mutability and mortality."[5]

Although the terms are different, this pattern of integrating different parts of the self to achieve balance, wisdom, is essentially the same as the Jungian model of individuation. We may object to the Jungian concept of the development of the self as the harmonization of the male and female principles (although it seems to me that these metaphors are also important for our culture), but basically the pattern of the two models is that of incorporating meaningful difference—terms which are related structurally to one another—into one's life.

This must be refined further, however, and in doing so, we expose one of the inadequacies of the Jungian model. The basic question is: Where does this element of "difference" come from? It is surely a mistake to think that the quality "wisdom" resides within the person, anymore than we are correct in saying that "such-and-such is cold" (it is cold only in relationship to something else). This insight reveals one of the fundamental difficulties in the Jungian model of individuation: the phenomenon of growth is presented as if it were automatically generated from within the psyche. It is not an accident that Jung uses the image of the philosophical tree to represent psychic growth, a metaphor that is misleading because it overemphasizes the automatic, programmed character of growth. And within the world of Jungian theory the role of art is to reveal the process which is working through it; art does not present the mind with new elements and problems to be dealt with. It is the degree of passivity that Jung's model implies that is inappropriate to a model of human growth and development.

In this regard, Erik Erikson's model of the unfolding stages of psychosocial development is superior, for it correctly emphasizes the give and take, the trial and error, which take place between the individual and society. (Parenthetically I should add that both theories are normative, which the intellectual community also objects to, and strenuously. This response too must be analyzed. We are understandably uncomfortable when we measure ourselves against stages of growth and find ourselves lacking. Yet the resistance to models of authority is too shrill, I believe. But this I must leave aside.) Although Erikson's model stresses socializing roles (the role of the adolescent, the parent, the worker, and so on), I find his model more useful than Jung's in accounting for the development of what we call wisdom because it does deal with the notion of learning (calibration, as Bateson calls it) as a systematic exchange between organism and environment, which we could define as the materials of one's art, as well as one's social world. Difference, in other words, does not so much come from within (although one must meet it with both rigor and imagination, if one is to learn anything or achieve anything of value), as it does from without. For Bateson—and I think he is right—this is a definition of creative thought: "*Creative* thought must always contain a random component. The exploratory processes—the endless *trial and error* of mental progress—can achieve the *new* only by embarking upon pathways randomly presented, some of which when tried are somehow selected for something like survival."[6]

As the above suggests, I do not agree with the cynical Yeats who asserted darkly that wisdom is a property of the dead. Nor by wisdom do I mean the maxims which we find in "The Wisdom of Solomon," or the *Ta Hio* of Confucius, although they are by no means irrelevant. Indeed some of the sayings, like the following from "The Wisdom of Solomon," are just now being "proved" by social gerontologists statistically: "If you have not gathered wisdom in your youth, / How will you find it when you are old?" Instead, I mean something much more abstract both in terms of the lives and art of these individual poets and the role their poetry plays in the larger domain of cultural history.

In closing this book, I take pleasure in referring to Hannah Arendt's splendid book *The Human Condition,* which I have had occasion to return to recently. In that model of lucid thought, Arendt traces our alienation in the modern world to the historical development of Western culture, which has reversed the hierarchical order between the *vita contemplativa* and the *vita activa*. Worse, the contemplative life—once the supreme value in human life—has been rendered valueless. This, she argues, is a perversion, for the contemplative life represents the highest, perhaps the purest, activity of which we are capable.

The late poems of these poets embody that which is lacking in our culture. The pursuit of the eternal—which is indeed what Pound, Eliot, and Williams, and even Stevens were devoted to—cannot be submitted to the coarse test of pragmatism. Contemplation, Arendt insists, is not the same as thought and reasoning. Contemplation is absolute quiet. Contemplation has as its goal beholding the truth. Wisdom has its source in solitude, although to be in solitude is to be with one's self, a partner. The still point. "Every movement," she writes, "the movements of body and soul as well as of speech and reasoning, must cease before truth. Truth, be it the ancient truth of Being or the Christian truth of the Living God, can reveal itself only in complete human stillness."[7] And these meditative poems testify to the nobility of the life of the mind as the quintessential human activity.

1. Gregory Bateson, *Mind and Nature: A Necessary Unity* (New York: E. P. Dutton, 1979), p. 201.

2. *Mind and Nature*, p. 200.

3. Letter from Wallace Stevens to Barbara Church, July 27, 1949, in *Letters*, p. 643.

4. Simone de Beauvoir, *The Coming of Age*, trans. Patrick O'Brian (New York: Warner Paperback Library, 1973), p. 60.

5. Herbert Blau, "Shadow Boxing: Reflections on the Tai Chi Ch'uan," in *Break Out: In Search of New Theatrical Environments*, ed. James Schevill (Chicago: Swallow Press, 1973), p. 362.

6. *Mind and Nature*, p. 182.

7. Hannah Arendt, *The Human Condition* (Chicago: University of Chicago Press, 1958), p. 15.

INDEX TO AUTHORS

INDEX TO WORKS DISCUSSED